BAYREUTH
African Studies Series

Publisher/Editor:

Eckhard Breitinger
Bayreuth University
D-95440 Bayreuth
Germany / R.F.A.

Price per copy:	DM 29,00; US $ 21.50; £ 11.95	(plus postage)
Cloth:	DM 44,90; US $ 34.50; £ 19.90	(plus postage)

ISBN 3-927510-27-0 / ISBN 3-927510-17-3 (cloth)
ISSN 0178-0034

Printed by D. Gräbner, D-96146 Altendorf

Foto: E. Breitinger

Jos 1983

Derek Wright

The Novels of Nuruddin Farah

Contents

PREFACE

This book is a comprehensive study of Nuruddin Farah's published novels in English. It does not deal, except in passing, with his non-fictional prose, his early novella, his part-published novel in Somali or his four unpublished plays. As is appropriate for a first work on an author, the book is written mainly at the level of a critical introduction and is designed to serve primarily at that level. The chapters on the *Dictatorship* trilogy and *Maps* occasionally venture into more arcane and recondite critical territory, consistent with the complex material of these novels. In my introduction I have tried, alongside a summary sketch of Somalia's complex cultural heritage and clan politics, to give a brief impression of the range of Farah's literary and intellectual influences, and in subsequent chapters have given some space to their intricate workings. The book is not intended, however, to be a work of searching background scholarship. A detailed and systematic investigation of the indigenous narrative, religious and linguistic sources of Farah's fiction is beyond the scope of the present study and the qualifications of its author, and is a task better left to Somali and Somali-speaking scholars with first-hand knowledge of the relevant traditions.

A note on spelling and naming. I have adhered throughout the text to the Italian spelling of the Somali capital favoured by the author: Mogadiscio, instead of the more fashionable Mogadishu. Somali nomenclature has become entangled in misconceptions and I do not wish to be caught up in the controversy. For convenience, I have referred to the author by the Westernized form of his name which appears on all his writings and which he has allowed to become the common and customary usage. Thus, rightly or wrongly, the "given" name Nuruddin (literally, "the light of religion") and the paternal name Farah are employed as loose equivalents of, respectively, the "Christian" name and the surname in the Western tradition.

Thanks are due to a number of people for aid in the composition and production of this book. I would like to express gratitude to Jacqueline Bardolph of the University of Nice for generously providing my research student and myself with copies of her essays and a manuscript copy of Farah's unpublished play *Yussuf and his Brothers*; to Ali Jimale Ahmed of Queens College, City University of New York, for some useful information supplied during our meeting at the MLA Conference in San Francisco in 1991; and to Abdulrazak Gurnah of the University of Kent for information of a more immediate and practical kind. I am indebted to my M.A. student Betty Oliver for her translations of foreign language articles and for sharing with me her knowledge of Islam and her enthusiasm for Farah's writing; and to my doctoral student Maggi Phillips for making available to me some useful material on the religious backgrounds to *Close Sesame*. Special thanks are also due to my graduate students Marina Deegan and John Sarev for their meticulous proof-reading of the manuscript, and to Maggi Phillips for the same; to Elaine Glover and Cathy Robertson of the Northern Territory University Library for their prompt acquisition of relevant secondary material; to Renate Mohrbach-Wright for her long-term support and encouragement; and to the Northern Territory University for a semester's leave from teaching, during which this book was written. Finally I would like to thank my editor and publisher Eckhard Breitinger for allocating a volume of his African Studies Series to one of Africa's most exciting contemporary novelists.

I wish to acknowledge the permission to quote from *From A Crooked Rib*, *A Naked Needle*, *Sweet and Sour Milk*, *Sardines*, *Close Sesame*, *Maps* and *Gifts* granted by the author and his agent Rogers, Coleridge and White Ltd., London. Extracts from *Gifts* appear with the permission of Serif Publishers, London, in association with Baobab Books Harare. I would also like to make grateful acknowledgment to Harper Collins for a quotation from *Wild Swans* by Jung Chang. Thanks are due to the editors of the following journals and presses for allowing me to reproduce some material contained, and presented in a different form, in articles originally published by them: *ARIEL* and the University of Calgary Board of Governors; *College Literature* and West Chester University Press; *The Journal of Commonwealth Literature* and Hans Zell Publishers; *Modern Fiction Studies* and the Purdue Research Foundation; *Research in African Literatures* and Indiana University Press; and *Studies in Twentieth Century Literature* and Kansas State University Press.

Darwin 1994

CHAPTER ONE
Introduction: Writer and Nation

Nuruddin Farah comes from an originally nomadic tradition and his travels, studies and employments have, appropriately, been nomadic on a global scale. These have taken him to England, Italy and Germany; to Canada and the United States; to India; and, on the African continent, to Nigeria, Gambia, Tunisia, Uganda and the Sudan. The preoccupying subject throughout his writing career, however, has been the oppression of his native Somalia by the totalitarian regime of General Muhammad Siyad Barre which was in power from 1969 to 1991. This Somalia, which he left in 1974 and in which his own works were banned for nearly two decades (though rumoured to have had an underground oral circulation), is the subject to which he has returned in novel after novel.

Nuruddin Farah Hassan[1] was born in 1945 in Baidoa in the Italian-administered south of the country, which on 1 July 1960 would be united with the northern territory of British Somaliland to form the independent republic of Somalia. He grew up in the town of Kallafo in the Ethiopian-ruled Ogaden and received his secondary education at Shashamanne School in Ethiopia, where he was taught mainly in Amharic and Arabic, and at the Institutio di Magistrale di Mogadisclo, where the language of instruction was Italian. After completing his secondary schooling he worked briefly in the Ministry of Education in the capital. At the age of twenty he wrote a novella, *Why Dead So Soon?*, from a hospital bed while awaiting an operation and had this published in a government-run newspaper in 1966. In the same year he left for India, where he spent the next four years studying for a B.A. in literature and philosophy at the Punjab University of Chandigarh. Here he married and wrote plays and revues, one of which was broadcast on India radio in 1968; he also completed the manuscripts of two apprentice-novels, both of which were rejected, and in March and April of 1968 wrote his first published novel *From a Crooked Rib* (1970). Farah returned to Somalia in 1970 to work as a teacher in Mogadiscio, first at secondary schools and then at the National University, and was initially caught up in the heady revolutionary idealism unleashed by Siyad Barre's Soviet-inspired coup of October 1969. In articles written at this time the young author took a positive view of the event and expressed a broad sympathy with the aims of the reform programs set in motion by the

Supreme Revolutionary Council, though in so doing Farah merely subscribed to the widespread feeling of relief at deliverance from nine years of civilian misrule which prevailed at the time. It will be convenient here to survey briefly both that period and the national revolution and dictatorship which followed.

Somalia's experiment with colonial models of parliamentary democracy in the decade after independence had not been a happy one. At first it seemed that parliamentary processes would blend well with traditionally egalitarian Somali political institutions. In practice, however, the decision-making processes in pastoral society were too anarchic and its political systems too unstratified to lend themselves to controlled representative democracy on the national level. The difficulties of political organization were compounded by administrative, linguistic and communication problems arising from the dual colonial heritage, the entrenchedly pastoral north having no immediate common bond with the more metropolitan-minded south. The most pervasive and insidious factor in the undermining of democratic processes, however, and the supreme impediment to national unity, was the Somali clan system. Though the Somalis are, ethnically and linguistically, one of the most homogeneous of Africa's populations, and one of the largest single ethnic blocks on the continent,[2] their politics have always been bedevilled by fierce and often fanatical clan divisions. In Somalia, Farah has said, "You are not a person but a member of a clan. My being a Somali matters outside Somalia. But when you are inside, your own clan demands that you become a member of that, and not of a large nation."[3] In Somalia political allegiances are determined by the patrilineage, the lines of alliance and division drawn up by genealogy, and neither parliamentary nor military governments have been able to construct a political system capable of transcending tribal enmities. During the 1950s bitter clan fighting in the north was barely contained by the British protectorate and, though there was a deliberate attempt during the run-up to independence to weaken clan solidarities by diversifying the composition of political parties (it was made illegal for them to bear tribal names), the dominant, all-pervasive element in the politics of the newly-formed republic remained the binding bond of the individual to his kin: a bond which opened a direct communication line from the nomad in the interior to the bureaucrat in the civil service and the politician in the National Assembly. In the 1960s the latter body was subsequently rife with nepotism and corrupt preferment; its deputies traded votes and favours for personal profit, turning democracy into mercenary anarchy; and wasteful sectionalism prevailed at all levels of government. Party politics finally collapsed into small group factionalism based on local lineage rivalries, and this trend reached its *reductio ad absurdam* in the 1969 election, in which a record number of 1,002 candidates, representing a monstrous 62 parties, contested 123 seats. To many Somalis the October coup of that year came as a welcome relief.[4]

Barre's Somali revolution made a promising beginning, addressing its mission statement to the nation's urgent development needs. Among its stated goals were economic independence and social betterment; sexual equality before the law; the elimination of corruption and clan nepotism, to be achieved by a national campaign against tribalism; and a war upon poverty, disease and ignorance. Implementation followed quickly in new laws granting women the same inheritance rights as men and imposing heavy fines and prison sentences for tribalistic actions, and in a variety of ambitious welfare actions, including youth training projects, work programs for the urban unemployed and resettlement schemes for famine-struck herdsmen. The most striking success was the 1973 urban literacy campaign which followed the government's provision, in 1972, of a long-awaited orthography for the national language (its rural counterpart the following year was less successful and had to be aborted due to the catastrophic famine of 1974).[5]

The euphoria of 1969 proved, however, to be short-lived and the darker side of the Barre regime soon became evident as coercion and terror were employed to safeguard reform and uphold the new equities. The urban literacy program was enforced by threats of career demotions and dismissals. In 1972 two generals were publicly executed on charges of plotting to overthrow the infant revolutionary state and in 1975 ten local sheiks met with the same fate for preaching against the new equal inheritance laws. With the influx of Russian personnel, the agencies of thought control multiplied apace. State censorship at home held information under tight control, while Somali embassies carefully monitored and reported the activities of Somali nationals abroad. The National Security Service, under a K.G.B.-trained police chief, kept government officials under surveillance, using spies, informers and *agents provocateurs* to denounce recalcitrants, and began to exercise arbitrary powers of arrest, torture and detention. There sprang up throughout the country political Orientation Centres for the vetting and indoctrination of civil servants.

These were followed by Revolutionary Youth Centres manned by Mao-style people's vigilantes or "Victory Pioneers" (the Green Guards of *Sweet and Sour Milk*), whose task was to instil revolutionary fervour and whose first loyalty, unsullied by atavistic tribal allegiances, was to the nation's leader. The Orientation and Youth Centres were decorated with pictures of the new trinity: Marx, Lenin and Siyad. A hagiographical cult of leadership quickly grew up around the Head of State, who was proclaimed in praise songs and panegyric speeches as father of the nation, divinely guided saviour of his people, and the omnipotent author of every national achievement. In two farcical rigged elections, in 1979 and 1986, he was officially "re-elected" by 99.9% of his subjects.

This leadership cult was not only alien to the egalitarianism of traditional nomadic culture but also sharply at odds with the brand of Islam that Siyad Barre professed to subscribe to. By emphasizing the ideals of communalism, brotherhood and the general welfare, Barre presented his "Scientific Socialism" as a secular extension of Koranic principles, and therefore fully compatible with Islam; to this end he undermined reactionary religious authority by dispossessing the mullahs of what little political power they still retained. Yet Islam, because of its pervasive influence on everyday life, has long been one of the most politically susceptible of religions, and its rigid laws and authoritative demands for obedience and submission have made it one of the most reactionary-prone, one easily manipulated by unscrupulous repressive regimes. It is also, one recent commentator has argued,[6] notoriously liable to infiltration by both pre-Islamic oral culture and non-Koranic lore, which combine to produce such a profusion of scriptures and attributed sayings that any number of bogus "official versions" can be reconstructed and passed off as orthodox ideology to serve devious political ends. Siyad Barre's strange confection of Islam and Marxism in fact contained little of either and was really more an extension of "Siyadism" than of socialism. Koranic texts were mined and bowdlerized for political slogans by the regime's ideologues and the praise-names of the Almighty redirected at the deified dictator, investing him with unlimited power and authority. The equal inheritance laws proved to be but a perfunctory sop to sexual equality: in practice, Koranic respect for the dignity of women and reverence of the bearing womb found few outlets for expression in the everyday life of post-revolutionary Somalia.

Barre's policy towards clan leadership, like that towards traditional religious authority, was to undermine it only to pervert it to his own ends.

Though no one dared utter it publicly, which would have been an indictable offence, it was public knowledge that the regime's Marxist and Islamic rhetoric was but camouflage for a power base built upon persistent clan and lineage loyalties and upheld by extremes of nepotism. After the power reshuffles of the mid-1970s the clandestine code name for the regime among its detractors was "M.O.D.": 'M' for the President's own patrilineage, 'O' for the Ogaden lineage of his mother, and 'D' for the Dulbahante lineage of his son-in-law, the head of the National Security Service. By the mid-1980s clan hegemony had narrowed to a family dynasty, the one-party state to one-man rule. Not only were more than half of all senior administrative positions and officer commissions filled by members of Barre's own Mareehaan clan and its client groups, but the country was effectively ruled by Barre's family, known as the "Gang of Five": the dictator, his formidable first wife, her eldest son, his cousin and his maternal brother. Once the revolutionary smokescreen of detribalization had cleared, Barre emerged as the arch-manipulator of the tangled web of kinship. Secure in the support of his own kinsmen, he was able from his position of strength to exploit other tribal alliances and antagonisms, trading promotions and preferments to play one clan off against another. His survivalist strategy was to keep the structure of inter-clan connections always open and unstable, and thence to paralyze resistance by reducing all would-be oppositional alliances to conditions of stalemate and deadlock. From 1971 to his eventual overthrow in the war-and-famine catastrophe of 1991, every attempted coup was thwarted by these highly successful divide-and-rule tactics. The 1978 attempt foundered in tribal parochialism and failed to gain national support, despite widespread public discontent after the Ogaden debacle. Neither the Somali Salvation Democratic Front nor the Somali National Movement of 1981 managed to live up to its name since both were clan-based movements (respectively, Majeerteen and Isaq) and therefore easily discredited as "tribalist" by the ruling tribal oligarchy.

The upshot of all this was that before it was a decade old the Somali revolution had already betrayed each of its original ideals and had earned for the country one of the worst human rights records on the African continent.[7] The last of its aims, the hitherto unmentioned goal of Pan-Somali irredentism, came to grief in the catastrophic 1977-78 war with Ethiopia over the Ogaden, a conflict which caused a dramatic *volte-face* in super-power alignments in the Horn of Africa and lost Somalia the patronage of one power-bloc without gaining that of the other. Meanwhile, inside the country the slide towards totalitarianism gathered pace. States of Emergency were declared, and the Supreme Revolutionary Council resurrected, in 1980 and 1986, during which police terror escalated and arrests and detention without trial became indiscriminate (in late 1981 over forty prominent professional figures in Mogadiscio were jailed on charges of subversion simply for trying to upgrade the quality of local public services). During these periods ministerial potentates like Farah's Soyaan and Samater in the trilogy of novels about dictatorship fell in and out of favour at the nepotistical whim of the dictator; they followed a precarious trajectory that might lead them from high office at any moment, either into exile as foreign ambassadors or to prison and the firing squad.

For Farah disillusionment with the revolution set in quickly, with the first execution of political opponents in late 1971 and the ensuing wave of secret after-midnight interrogations and detentions from which the author himself was not exempt.[8] Of this period he has written:

> Yes, the days were noisy as violent tides; and the nights were filled with frightened whispers of people listening for the footsteps of the National Security Service men who were sure to come at dawn to arrest them, to humiliate them, to take away the husband from the wife, the son from his parents, the bread from the breadwinner.[9]

Invited on his return by the regime to "write something favourable about the revolution," Farah responded with his 1969 play *A Dagger in Vaccuum*, which was rejected by the censors as "scandalously unrevolutionary,"[10] and then, in 1973, he published an extract from a short novel in Somali (the first novel to be written in the language), which the authorities declared seditious and halted the serialization of. At this time many members of the westernized urban elite who had been prominent in the civilian politics of the previous decade fled the country to escape harassment and detention by the security service and it was not long before Farah joined this "brain-drain." He departed the country in August 1974, leaving behind a young son, and spent the next two years in England pursuing postgraduate work in Theatre Studies at the Universities of London and Essex; during this period he was also attached for eight months to the Royal Court Theatre in London. At the University of Essex he was allowed to submit a play, *The Offering*, in lieu of an M.A. thesis but left without completing the course and the degree was not conferred. During Farah's residence in England the B.B.C. in London considered three of his plays for radio and in December 1978 broadcast one of them, *A Spread of Butter*, on the B.B.C. African Service.

Farah was about to return to Somalia in 1976 when, as the result of a fortuitous phone call to his brother from the transit lounge in Rome airport, he learned that his recently published novel *A Naked Needle* (1976) had fallen foul of the government. A chance meeting in the airport with the Somali Minister of Justice, who warned him that a jail sentence of thirty years awaited him in Mogadiscio, confirmed that it was not safe to return. Subsequently, Farah remained in Rome for the next three years and worked on *Sweet and Sour Milk* (1979) and *Sardines* (1981), the first and second volumes of the trilogy *Variations on the Theme of an African Dictatorship*; this sequence of novels was completed by *Close Sesame* (1983), written during a six months stay at the University of Bayreuth, Germany, in 1981. Since then Farah has lived and worked in a succession of African countries - *Maps* (1986) and the play *Yussuf and his Brothers* (performed 1982) were written in Nigeria, *Gifts* (1992) in the Gambia - and has interspersed his periods of African residence with brief visits to Europe and North America (he has held temporary teaching fellowships at UCLA, the State University of New York, and the Universities of Connecticut and Minnesota). He currently divides his time between Nigeria and England; in twenty years he has not returned to his native Somalia, though he has lived close to its frontiers (in Uganda and in the Sudan), and has always denied that he is in exile, except in the immediate physical sense:

> I am not the one who is in exile; it is the leaderships, the dictators of Africa that are in exile. I may be absent physically, but I am not absent spiritually nor am I exiled from my own people who, to the best of my knowledge, have a high respect for the principles by which I stand, and still retain their trust in me.[11]

"In Africa writing is a matter of life and death," Farah has said. "If you write something condemnatory of the regime in power they pass the death sentence on your head."[12] The violence and terror of recent Somali history are the proper formative contexts for his view of the writer as "the creator and shaper of the nation's enlightened opinion," "the trustee to the nation's wishes," and of "social commitment" and "social comment" as "the primary forces which make a writer write."[13] Farah's commitment to human freedom is a desperate one but it is also a balanced and discriminating one, a non-partisan, non-aligned engagement that has challenged the orthodoxies of both Right and Left: "The only thing one can do is to be aware and to struggle harder and harder against repression in whatever form it comes - whether traditionally in the form of a patriarch, religiously or in wearing the masks of an alien ideology."[14] Repression in Farah's fiction derives from a variety of sources - Africa and the West, the collusions of family and state authoritarianisms, the negative collaboration of tribalism, Islam and Marxism - and each of them is regarded with the same fair-minded vigilance and equanimity. Nothing is rejected outright, no party exonerated or blamed; rather, every position is tested for whatever support it lends to independence of thought and unfudged moral judgement, a process which involves giving equal voice to opponents: "I like to give even the people whom I disapprove of a chance for their words to be heard."[15] Always, great care is taken to preserve this balance. For example, in his *Dictatorship* trilogy, Farah does not look to the communal ethics and group-economics of the traditional past for sanctuary from contemporary post-colonial evils; rather, he reveals how traditional communal values have become props for familial and tribal parasitism and for clan tyranny in the present. Yet neither does he reject these corporate values in favour of an isolationist Western individualism. The Western nuclearized family that displaces the extended kinship group in this sequence of novels is shown to develop subtle new tyrannies of its own, and its principal champion, Medina in *Sardines*, wonders whether her education in foreign ideologies and cosmopolitan values has not rendered her a guest in her own country, unqualified to criticize what she sees. At the political level the General, no doubt, answers to some authentic need in the Somali experience, but it is, Farah insists, foreign powers - first Russia, then America - who help to keep him in power. In the trilogy's profile of dissident elements, ranging from the youthful Koschin to the aging Deeriye, neither Westernized nor "traditional" protagonists have a monopoly on opposition to the General's rule.

The same impartiality and sense of dual possibilities inform Farah's treatment of the oral tradition. Societies that rely chiefly on oral modes of communication and have few written records are ripe for political abuse by obscurantist dictators like the General, and due emphasis is given to this point in *Sweet and Sour Milk*. But Farah also stresses the richness of the oral culture's poetic traditions, together with their strength and vitality as sources of public commitment and independent-minded criticism. In Somalia poets have always been very visible and controversial figures, preeminent in the daily lives of the people and the social issues affecting them, and, in their acclaimed political duels and debates, a polemical force in the regulation of public opinion. Somali oral tradition is not fossilized in the past but is a dynamic influence, contemporaneous with the present in which it is constantly renewed, and an empowering agent for the preservation of the culture's most valuable assets.[16] Thus, when public debate and criticism were stifled during the clampdowns of the 1980s Emergencies, the oral culture acted as a spontaneous, alternative organ of protest, circulating in cassette form a series of vitriolic poetic attacks on the nation's leaders. The oral poet, however, is not a private voice but speaks with the collective tongue of the group: he has, says Farah, "a social function as the mouthpiece of the clan," [17] and this function may be used to enlarge or to restrict awareness. It has been observed, for example, that while the art of some traditional sheikh-poets, such as Wiil-Waal and the Sayyid, was a progressive force, cutting radically across clan lines, other "keepers of the word" used their craft to reinforce monopolistic and reactionary power-bases within the clans.[18] Many of the oral poets who, in the early 1970s, took upon themselves the task of presenting to the nation the Supreme Revolutionary Council's principles and aims soon found themselves parrotting government propaganda and composing sycophantic praise-songs to the leader and his lineage (these praise-singers are satirized in *Sweet and Sour Milk*). Accordingly, Farah's trilogy presents the oral tradition as a double-edged sword, by turns liberal and conservative, radical and reactionary, in its uses.

Farah is one of Africa's most multi-lingual, multi-cultural and multi-literate writers. At the age of ten he knew, in addition to spoken Somali, four language-scripts: the Amharic script of his school in the Ogaden; the Arabic script of the Koranic school; the Roman script of the two colonial languages, English and Italian; and Cusmanniya, an underground Somali script and symbol of Somali nationhood which in the Ogaden was learned secretly because of the disapproval of both the Ethiopian and European colonial authorities. At thirteen he had read Dostoevsky and Victor Hugo in Arabic and English translations. "We moved from one language universe to another," he has written, "with the disquiet of a tenant on a temporary lease."[19] But the effect was not only disquieting but dislocative and alienating, for all the textbooks used in the Somali-speaking Ogaden - the Arabic or Amharic ones and the English language ones borrowed from British colonies in East Africa - were meant for other national and ethnic groups: "the textbooks we were taught from belonged in the mind and culture of other people."[20] From these rival aliens Farah chose English as his medium of expression: apart from the aborted novel in Somali, all of his works - his seven novels, four plays and numerous essays - are written in this language. English is in fact his fourth tongue and would appear to be an unusual choice for a Somali writer but, as Farah has explained, he opted for English chiefly in order to reach a wide audience, both European and African, and rejected Somali (which had no orthography when he began writing) because of its technical deficiencies and inadequacies in the face of the complexities of the late twentieth-century world.

Farah's literary and intellectual influences are legion and can only be dealt with summarily here. First, if only in the chronological sense, there is the oral tradition. Farah comes from a family of oral poets (two great-grandfathers and his mother, who died in 1990, were poets) and although, as an anglophone writer working in the Western form of the novel, he has crossed the bridge between the oral and written traditions, there is still a sense in which his own writing *is* the bridge: that is, insofar as it self-consciously incorporates elements of orature within itself. Ebla's hesitant, reflective, improvisatory style of narrative in *From a Crooked Rib* is the most obvious link between the two traditions but the ornate, baroque elements of style in the later work also owe something to Somali oral poetry, particularly that of Farah's native Ogaden, which is famous for its imagistic richness and lush verbal ornamentation, its use of parallelism, veiled allusion and allegoric motif. The virtuoso alliteration and onomatopoeia which are such powerful mnemonics in the traditional *gabay* are much in evidence in Koschin's narrative in *A Naked Needle*, while elements of riddle, fable and symbolism as used in the *heello* have clearly left their mark on the mysterious epigraphic passages that open the chapters in *Sweet and Sour Milk*.[21] Of equal importance to the fiction is Arabic literature, both classical and modern, to which Farah has admitted debts and affinities (though, surprisingly perhaps, none of his own work has been translated into Arabic). Inevitably, in the work of a writer who is culturally Muslim, the Koran is a pervasive influence, an inexhaustible reference-source and touchstone, the scriptural references that punctuate the trilogy serving as important yardsticks for the General's illegitimate uses of Islam. Farah's most Islamic work, *Close Sesame*, is saturated with Koranic lore and Caliphate history, and is loosely structured around the pattern of the Suras, each part of the novel beginning with Deeriye's morning prayers and benedictions to "the most merciful and most compassionate" Lord.

Additionally, Farah has acknowledged the influence of *The Arabian Nights* upon his fiction, confessing his enthusiasm for "anecdotes tied together neatly by the one who narrates" and "the idea of having a story within the story, the idea of an endless debate with oneself, the idea of the allegorical nature of the tale itself, and of the flowery aspect of language [...]"[22] The conventional moralistic and homiletic aspects of *The Arabian Nights* are evident enough in the fiction: the "teaching-stories" from the oral culture which Deeriye narrates to Samawade in *Close Sesame*, and Misra to Askar in *Maps*, work in much the same way as those told by Scheherazade to Shahryar. But the principal debts to the Arabic classic, as Farah's interview comments indicate, are formal and stylistic rather than didactic. *The Arabian Nights* is perhaps best known for its plenitude of narrative strategies and inventions and its encyclopaediac combination of genres (witness Farah's conflation of detective novel, political thriller and *nouveau roman* in *Sweet and Sour Milk*), together with a range of formal elements that are recognizable among the ingredients of Farah's fiction. These include the labyrinthine plot structures, the intricate play of analogic motif, the predilection for serial, discontinuous narrative sequences over "one-off" creations, and the imbricated patterns of parallelism and counterchange: as the chapter titles of this study suggest, Farah delights in the "doubling" or pairing off of members of different families - mothers and daughters in *Sardines*, fathers and sons in *Sweet and Sour Milk* and *Close Sesame* - in order to explore patterns of likeness in unlikeness, uniformity in diversity. Recent critics have also regarded the peculiarly open-ended, indefinite structure and multi-layered reflexiveness of *The Arabian Nights* as potential models for avant-garde Modernism and its successors, citing among the fabulations of Borges, Rushdie and Angela Carter the work of Farah himself.[23] In these writings, as in Farah's, the ancient and the postmodern join hands.

Farah's fiction, of course, bears the marks of wide reading in Western literature, especially the Moderns, and this aspect of his work has received some critical attention. The novels abound with epigraphs and quotations from Conrad, Beckett, Kafka, Brecht and Yeats; there is a strong Joycean presence in the diurnal narrative and stylistic extravagances of Koschin's narrative in *A Naked Needle*; and the play of leit-motif (what Farah has called "the internal structures of ideas")[24] is abundant throughout the fiction. What critical commentators have been slower to recognize, however, are the resemblances which elements of Farah's writing bear to the standard features of postmodernist fiction. Notable among these are the novels' narrative inconclusiveness, often petering out in mid-plot; the conspicuous and ingenious play of parallelism; and the collapsing of ontological boundaries by multiple, superimposed orders of reality. As in postmodernist fiction, there is no attempt at a complete view of character, only a series of reported versions; and fragmented, composite characters - spaces inhabited by multiple presences - are favoured over unitary personalities. Characters have "transworld" identities, reappearing in novel after novel, though sometimes with the arbitrary indeterminacy of Robbe-Grillet's or John Barth's creations rather than the realistic consistency of Balzac's or Faulkner's. As regards this recycling of characters, or *retour de personnages*,[25] it is worth noticing that, although on one level there is maintained the realistic illusion of the characters' continuing lives outside the texts, their essential properties as individuals seldom carry over from one text to another (Medina, Margaritta and Dulman are merely names in the novels where they make no appearances), and characters do not always correspond unequivocally with their intertextual signifiers: the mature Ebla of *Sardines* seems to have little continuity with the adolescent Ebla of the earlier *From a Crooked Rib*, and there is no reliable evidence that the "Ladan" and "Sagal" who join the gathering in Natasha's kitchen at the end of *Close Sesame* are, respectively, Loyaan's sister in *Sweet and Sour Milk* and Ebla's daughter in *Sardines*. Sometimes, as in the case of the government spy Ahmed-Wellie, the truth about a character is not learned, nor his inconsistencies ironed out, until the third book in which he appears; sometimes, as in the case of Mulki in *Sweet and Sour Milk*, nothing can ultimately be known about the character, whose very existence is left in doubt and who therefore has no more than nominal status. The result is that the fictional ontology is alternately reinforced and destabilized, and the novels' intertextuality is of both the illusionist and the anti-illusionist kind. Furthermore, as Ian Adam has observed, Farah's compulsive patterning of his people into pairs, establishing bold identifications between rival parents and children, domestic and political patriarchs, victims and avengers, teachers and pupils, at times puts the Western reader in mind of the alternative mirror-worlds or parallel universes that feature so prominently in postmodern science-fiction.[26]

In some of the novels these postmodern tendencies are contained, their excesses held in check within traditional illusionist modes. In *Sardines*, for example, the solipsistic mentalities of characters like Medina and Sagal are realistically framed, the paranoia politically placed. The uncertainties that beset them are mainly of the epistemological kind, the outcome of ideological fixations, rival rumoured versions of the same event, and speculative reconstructions of motives. And in the twilight world of *Close Sesame* the relations of reality and metaphor turn on a fine but firm line - between, for example, the mysterious Khaliif's literal madness and his symbolic sanity. In *Sweet and Sour Milk*, however, it is the individual's ontological grip on the world that is at stake, a hold which is rendered doubly insecure by the vagaries of the oral code and the mystificatory practices of an obscurantist political regime. The questions raised here are ones of existence rather than identity: what is uncertain is not who but what and *if* people are. In this novel we are squarely back in the postmodern literary terrain and in *Maps*, the first book written after the completion of the trilogy, Farah returns to the same territory. In *Maps* sexual, national and ontological boundaries are straddled by the protagonist in such a way as to dissolve the distinctions between the things they divide. In this novel what has formerly served, in the trilogy, as a merely analogic or imaginative order is actualized and the frontier is collapsed into the border territory of the mind, where the imaginary and fantastic are made fact, metaphors literal, the surreal real. "Every image floats vaguely in a sea of doubt," runs the novel's Conradian epigraph: on the dreamscapes of *Maps* everything is of transitional and indeterminate identity, melting from one form into another.

Nuruddin Farah is thus a man of many parts, an author with access to many languages, cultures and literatures which react in combination to produce a volatile fictional chemistry. He has lived in many parts of Africa, and can thus claim to speak for, and to derive his inspiration from, the whole continent - "Africa is the neurosis around which my creativity grows"[27] - and when he does speak, it is in many voices and styles:

> A writer [...] is in a sense everybody. He is a woman, he is a man. He is as many other selves as those whose shadows reflect his ghostly images; he is as many other selves as the ones whose tongues he employs to articulate his thoughts; he is as many other selves as there are minds and hearts he dwells in.[28]

His novels are forums of debate which "allow very many different competing views to be heard,"[29] in the hope that truth will issue from the collision of opposing ideas; for truth in Farah's fiction is relative, ambiguous and open-ended. There is no final commitment to any single point of view in these multi-layered works, only a succession of narrative voices and viewpoints: those of young girl and old man, infant and adolescent, African and Westerner, Somali and Pan-Somali, male and female - and, in *Maps*, the multi-generic ("the woman's self in the man, the man's self in the woman").[30] Farah, like each of his protagonists from Ebla and Koschin to Askar and Duniya, is a liminal phenomenon, one who crosses boundaries and migrates between zones. He is an oddity among African artists, unique in his contradictions: a nomad and a cosmopolitan; a man from a land of oral poets who writes fiction; a Somali author who lives outside his homeland yet, obsessively, writes about no other subject (though not in Somali); and that rarity in African literature, a male author who writes with a profound and enduring sympathy for women.

But then the Somalis are themselves something of an oddity in the modern world and are equally unstable of definition and classification. Koschin, who dubs them a "Country of Curiosity" in the early novel *A Naked Needle*, explains:

> An Englishman in the colonial days [...] is supposed to have said that Somalis are like Epsom salt, which spurts, foams and settles to the bottom in the time it takes to bat your eyelids. [...] I suppose he was right, for we are a people that need constant changes in government, in leadership. We rise, we revolt against any power and eventually tend to accept it as our fate. We are a very subordinate folk, easy to govern. In short, we are a people of God.[31]

Sixteen years on, Farah comes to terms with another set of contradictions:

> The 'truth' that there is nothing unique about them has upset them greatly. [...] This has been unsettling to the Somalis who generally lack a centrally organized form of opposition, of resistance. [...] In consequence, they have scattered themselves to the winds, making a study of their character difficult, cumbersome, almost impossible. When in exile, they long to get back home: home to a notion of Somalia, commonly accepted to be the guiding principle of its people; when at home, they are eager to get away from the promiscuity of the-Somali-idea, the particularity of the Somalis' world view.[32]

The question of the Somalis' supposed uniqueness is not settled by either of these somewhat tongue-in-cheek speakers, but their voices bear common testimony to the inconstant, unpredictable nature of the Somali temperament and worldview, a volatile quality which is reflected in the country's wayward post-independence history. Since its establishment in 1960, the Somali republic has shifted its political alignments and allegiances with a perverse frequency. The denizens of the new nation-state have been a people of uncertain orientation, neither this nor that, neither here nor there: socialist, yet patriarchal; ethnically homogeneous, yet rent by the incestuous micro-tribalisms of clan and lineage; fragmented by diaspora in the Horn of Africa but inveterately irredentist in their sense of a Pan-Somali identity; an African people neither of the Maghrib nor black Africa; an Islamic people who, though having strong historical ties with the Arab world and speaking a language abundant with Arab loan-words, have since the 1969 Revolution alienated the conservative, wealthier Arab states with which geography, religion and culture have given them the closest ties. It would be unusual if a body of fiction devoted to the career of this country over the last twenty years did not tap its rich mine of contradictions and issue in a complex and difficult artistic achievement. I will endeavour to do some justice to that achievement in the following pages.

CHAPTER TWO
A Wife and Her Husbands: *From a Crooked Rib*

From a Crooked Rib was not only Farah's first novel but the first novel by a Somali writer. Set in the colonial 1950s, it focuses on the uneducated nomadic woman Ebla, her attempts to escape patriarchal tyranny and her bid for whatever little independent identity her period of national history will allow. When it was published in 1970 its marked sympathy for oppressed Somali womanhood made it a unique, pioneering piece of African fiction.

At the beginning of the novel the nineteeen-year-old Ebla is promised in marriage by her grandfather, without her consent, to the forty-eight year old Giumaleh. Her response is to flee the *Jes*, her local kinship group, thus ending both its legal ownership and protection of her (for this her grandfather curses and wishes death on her, though he is the one who dies). Stepping out of her nomadic pastoral community for the first time in her life, Ebla joins a caravan to the town of Belet-Wane, where she is taken in by a male cousin, the storekeeper Gheddi, but only to receive much the same treatment from him as from her grandfather. Gheddi sells her hand to his creditor Dirir, a man dying of tuberculosis, but not before he has made use of her as an impromptu midwife to deliver his son, as a servant, and as a courier for smuggled goods: when the smugglers are caught by the colonial police, it is the unfortunate Ebla, seen by Gheddi as "an ominous person," who is blamed and promptly evicted. In order to escape this second forced match, Ebla is persuaded by a local widow to elope to Mogadiscio with the young Italian-educated civil servant and teacher Awill. It transpires, however, that Awill, though promising marriage, is merely seeking a permanent sexual partner as an alternative to prostitutes. On her first traumatic evening in the capital Ebla, virginal and circumcised, is beaten and, in a manner that is more rape than seduction, is laboriously and painfully deflowered. The next morning, with the aid of a couple of local sheikhs, she is duly and gullibly "married" (the word is problematic in the context of this novel), and Awill, without so much as a farewell, promptly flies off to a study tour in Italy, where he acquires an Italian mistress. After seeing a photograph of Awill and the white woman together, the ingenuous Ebla decides to revenge herself upon him by entering into a new "marriage," this time to the rich businessman Tiffo, another sexual predator in search of a single night's gratification. The sheikhs are again called upon and the next day, when Tiffo correctly suspects that his termagant first wife has found out about Ebla, they are called back to legitimize the divorce. At the end of the book Awill returns from Italy convinced, to his surprise, that he feels genuine affection for Ebla in spite of his mistreatment of her. As the sun sets on the capital the novel ends enigmatically: Awill, who is "as usual, hot with desire," is received back into her bed by Ebla, who takes pity upon him - "Poor fellow, he needs me. He is sex-starved" - and forgivingly welcomes "his hot and warm world into her cool and calm kingdom."[1]

As Ebla makes her picaresque outward passage from desert camp to small town and metropolis, there is no corresponding progression or expansion in the spectrum of male attitudes to women, which remains oppressively narrow. Spinsters, says one of the anonymous male visitors at Gheddi's house, "come in handy when one needs a woman to marry" (p. 50). Awill, like Gheddi before him, speaks to such visitors in Ebla's presence as if she were deaf or absent. When Ebla defiantly asserts her equality with Tiffo - "You have another wife and I have another husband" - his response is: "We are not equal. You are a woman and you are inferior to me. And if you have another husband, you are a harlot" (p. 145). Islamic law enshrines a double-standard of morality which permits Awill to marry and bring home as many as four women if he wants, but declares the women prostitutes if they dare to reciprocate. "God created Woman from a crooked rib," runs the novel's titular epigraph, "and any one who trieth to straighten it, breaketh it," and the traditional proverb, Biblical but in fact unKoranic,[2] is restated by Awill on the last page of the book. Woman, not the world in which she moves, is deemed innately bent and askew. She is a flawed creature, born with a crooked back, destined to receive whatever burden is placed upon it, and impossible to "straighten" or make perfect.

The feminist concerns of the later *Dictatorship* trilogy (especially *Sardines*) and of *Maps* are already close to the surface in the tale of Ebla's determined flight from bartered marriages with elders and consumptives in a society where a woman's only alternative to being sold by others as a chattel-wife is to sell herself as a prostitute. Indeed, there is a very thin line between the two institutions in the novel and Farah's point, according to one critic, is that "the structure of the Somali family makes prostitutes of all Somali women."[3] In the kinship group depicted here women, whether for sex or domestic service, are bought and sold into marriage like beasts: they are, in fact, worth only their exchange value in cattle and camels in the form of the bride-price fixed by the patriarch, though, characteristically, their contribution to the family's wealth in this way is seldom acknowledged.[4] Women, the widow in Belet-Wane explains to Ebla, are always male properties in some sense, whether of fathers, husbands or cousins, and as such are disposable commodities. Ebla reflects that "girls were materials just like objects, or items on the shelf of a shop" and to a shopkeeper there is no "difference between a girl and his goods" (p. 84). Though Ebla is sustained by the conviction that she is a "wife" of some sort, she is not a wife in any meaningful sense of the word and none of her four "husbands" are worthy of the name. She flees from two aborted arranged marriages, in which her word is given by a male relative without consulting her, to two marriages of doubtful legitimacy. The truth - that "she had become a prostitute without realizing that she had become one" (p. 161) - dawns only very slowly upon Ebla. She persists in the illusion that she is "master of myself," when she is the mistress of two men, and continues to think of herself as genuinely "married" and "divorced." In fact, the farcical speed with which these instant overnight-marriages and divorces are executed effectively transforms her into a sexual hireling, while the sheikhs who are paid to ratify the transactions are her virtual pimps and the landlady Asha her procuress. Correspondingly, Ebla is ingenuously promiscuous in her "wifehood" - "I love to be a wife. I don't care whose" (p. 125) - and, like a prostitute, she equates her sexual parts with her "bank."

Somali marriage, in Farah's polemical vision, is commercial, mercenary, exploitative. And yet, however unsatisfactory it may be, it remains the given condition through which everything in the woman's existence - even her strivings after individuality and independence - has to be expressed, and those who remain outside it, such as the widow and Asha, suffer the various punitive stigmas of spinsterhood (one is accused of loose morals, the other of greed). Ebla reflects: "She had run from the country to a town, and from there to Mogadiscio. Now if she ran from Mogadiscio, she would run into the ocean. [...] She had escaped before: it was no longer an enigma - the only problem was where to go" (pp. 83, 123). The Somali woman has no place to go, nowhere to run except into another marriage: "I love life, and life lies in marriage" (p. 126). Farah has said that at the time of writing he was interested in people who are deprived of what they cannot exist without, in the personal struggle for survival,[5] and in the Somalia of the first novel marriage is the principal and, in some cases, the only means of survival. The combined constraints of tribal patriarchy, Islamic law and the hardships of nomadic pastoralism ensure that only in marriage is there financial security and space (albeit limited) for self-definition. Thus Ebla, who "loves to be a wife," tests her individualistic aspirations within the framework of the institution, challenging her polygamous husbands with polyandrous experiments of her own. The latter, however, are short-lived and provide little relief from her plight, for simply to *be* a wife in Somali society is to call into play reactionary conventions that degrade and enslave women and is thus to reinforce one's subjugated status.

From the illiterate Ebla to the intellectual Medina, the women in Farah's fiction who attempt to take control of their destinies, either by trying to live outside the patriarchal structure or by modifying it from within, find their path blocked by insurmountable obstacles. They each discover that neither Somalia's slow evolution away from a pastoral nomadic past nor (as in Awill's case) foreign education and travel have done much to erode deeply entrenched cultural convictions of male superiority and female subservience. The independent-minded woman of the 1950s is subsequently driven into marginal groups of propertied widows, landladies, spinsters, divorcees and prostitutes which anticipate the isolated feminist fringe of the 1970s as depicted in the second novel of the *Dictatorship* trilogy. After making a brief appearance as a shop-keeper in *A Naked Needle*, Ebla next turns up twenty years later, serenely independent and prosperous from her divorces, in the nearly all-female cast of *Sardines*, where she is loosely attached, through her daughter Sagal, to Medina's circle. We learn in *Sardines* that Ebla later divorced Awill and inherited money from the man she married after him, and this hindsight knowledge of her fate tends, in fact, to problematize the ending of *From a Crooked Rib*. The Ebla of *Sardines*, the worldly-wise liberated matron, has clearly been educated by her city experiences and has profited from the pragmatic lessons learned from her marriages and divorces. In the light of this, it is not clear whether her resumption of her marital relationship with Awill at the end of the earlier novel should be seen as entry into a renewed sexual slavery or whether the closing reference to Ebla's sexual "kingdom" signifies that she is now in control and that traditional conventions have been transcended by a new understanding and mutual honesty: "We will tell each other everything tomorrow" (p. 179). The novel peters out problematically, making it hard to say exactly what kind of resolution, if any, has been achieved - whether Ebla's "crooked rib" stands straight and is entirely her own or whether it is permanently bent into servitude to another. The most likely explanation now seems that the later Ebla was unforeseen at this stage and that her integration into the novel-series was an afterthought rather than a planned move, so that the ending of the first book needs to be taken on its own independent terms.

Written in less than a month when its author was a twenty-three year old student in India, Farah's first novel is a piece of apprentice fiction which bears some of the marks of its hasty composition: notably, the slight story line and stylistic ineptitudes, the amount of repetition and redundant local colour, the narrative inconsistencies and vagaries of viewpoint. For example, after taking great care to keep intact Ebla's viewpoint from the Prologue on, he suddenly breaks into her narrative at the end of Chapter 17 to give the reader an "inside view" and interposed sexual history of Awill to explain how he comes to be here with her in the widow's house (the maneuver is repeated with Tiffo). Admittedly, Ebla's guileless view of the world, and her Clarissa-like innocence as she drifts unsuspectingly into prostitution, are well sustained for the greater part of the book. The plain, unadorned prose style captures perfectly her naive, untutored consciousness and registers exactly her wide-eyed wonder at the urban world of cars and aeroplanes, radios and bank accounts, spaghetti and Arab purdah-women: she thinks that "Police" and "Government" are the names of tribes and measures the period of Awill's absence in Italy as "180 milking-instances." And yet - perhaps inevitably, given his own situation and outlook - Farah's approximation of his ingenuous heroine's mental vocabulary is at best uneven and there are moments when his own more cultivated voice and educated phrasing break through to destroy the illusion ("discrimination between the sexes," "emotional make-up," "the ditch of matrimony," "one lived a parody of existence").

More seriously, the young author, only too aware of the novelty of his subject and the pioneering quality of his writing, allows his feminist special pleading to become noticeably strident in places:

> Why is it only the sons in the family who are counted? For sure this world is a man's - it is his dominion. It is his and is going to be his as long as women are oppressed, as long as women are sold and bought like camels, as long as this remains the system of life. Nature is against women. (p. 84)

This polemical tendency invests Ebla with spontaneous, intuitive notions of independence that appear uncharacteristic of an uneducated nomadic woman of her tradition and time, and issues in thoughts that are sometimes too great for the thinker. For Ebla examines not only her personal plight but the position of women in a male society, and she states the case for the equality, complementarity and mutual dependence of the sexes in terms that are transparently informed by Western ideas about individual freedom of choice:

> One thing they could not pay for is my indispensability. I am a woman. And I am indispensable to man [...] life meant freedom, freedom of every sort. One should do whatever one wants to - that is life. That is what I love. (pp. 106, 126)

Farah adds the qualifier, "She was unique in forming ideas about things" (p. 126), and the reflective style that he employs for her narrative becomes more successful as she becomes more of a thinking creature and has more thoughts to be reported. But this does not answer the crucial question which Ebla puts to herself at the outset: "Why do we think differently from the way we behave?" (p. 18). How does a woman of Ebla's background come to think in the way that she does? Not only are her ratiocinative powers occasionally ill at ease with her adolescent ingenuousness; her innate individualism is more deeply and inexplicably at odds with the laws of her cultural environment. Farah said in the 1989 interview, "A Combining of Gifts," that the great physical distances that separate traditional nomadic hamlets in Somalia have developed a strong sense of individualism and self-reliance in their inhabitants.[6] But, even allowing for such factors, Ebla's qualities of mind and independent disposition still distinguish her perhaps too markedly from everyone around her and, in the view of some commentators, make her too exceptional a creature to be entirely convincing.[7] The author seems to be partly aware of the extent to which his own emancipated ideas interfere with his heroine's autonomy and, perhaps to forestall criticism, covers himself at the outset with the rather weak disclaimer: "She thought of many things a woman of her background would never think of" (p. 8).

And yet, whatever the theoretical impediments to her character, Ebla remains a believable creation at the practical level of the reading experience. This is so, essentially, because she lives on the page as an oral being, triumphantly alive in an oral culture glimpsed here in its original unsullied state before its corruption by the General. The quirky, disjointed style of the narrative catches her living minute by minute, on the spot, improvising; pausing, in the manner of the oral tale, to examine the meaning of her experiences and the truth of her reflections on them; and expressing by turns a range of responses (credulity, curiosity, tolerance, amused contempt) none of which have any final or enduring value. Though uninformed, Ebla's is a shrewd and sceptical intelligence, and her medley of psychological "asides" shows how its instinctive wisdoms and insights are fed by remembered anecdotes and proverbs, folk tales and moral fables, and the poems of the Sayyid, all imbibed with the oral culture of her childhood. This oral mode sometimes issues in rustic commonplaces ("What is life if one outlives it?"), sometimes in ornate extended similes of great poetic ingenuity:

> Outside, the morning was lonely as if it were a widow whose second husband had just died and who intended never to re-marry but to face hardship and loneliness. The wind was sad as if it were a poor student whose ink-bottle had just broken into pieces and whose ink had coloured the ungrateful ground. The trees were standing apart as if they were afraid of each other and as if they would contaminate each other had they shaken and touched. Silence was the only refuge they all knew. That was the only language they could comprehend. The morning did not expect to be followed by another morning and another morning and another morning. The wind was glad to be sad for a change, maybe just as the student would be glad at breaking the bottle of ink to give him a legitimate excuse to stay outside the school premises. The trees were delighted to stay apart lest they should multiply and quarrel over space.
>
> Ebla had reached a decision in the meantime. She murmured to herself something she herself did not quite understand.
>
> 'Destiny and fate can be worked out,' she told herself. 'One dies only once, and only when one's Time comes. Nobody knows when Time will knock on his door. And when It does, It will be welcome. But until tomorrow, let me try to tackle my problem.' (p. 15)

As is common in oral poetry, the epic simile is really a disguised exemplum: behind it lies the pragmatic message that Ebla must start from where she is, making the best of her situation, the most positive use of her predicament. From Ebla to Dulman (and on to Misra in *Maps*) the strength and vitality of this oral tradition, resident in mainly female circles of protest, will be abiding forces in Farah's fiction.

In the aforementioned 1989 interview Maya Jaggi suggested to Farah that Ebla is a symbolic analogue for Somalia on the eve of independence, her various polyandric marriages mirroring the nation's oppressive relations with imperial masters, and this aspect of the novel has received some attention from critical commentators.[8] Certainly, references to the coming independence punctuate the novel, which ends portentously a month before the transfer of power, and in the last chapter Ebla expresses a number of virtuously anti-colonial sentiments, accusing Awill of aping patterns of Western commerce and consumerism. She is at this time pregnant with a child whose paternity is as uncertain as the nation's destiny, which may lie with any or none of its influential Italian, British and Ethiopian colonial fathers (the new nation, like the child and its mother's political consciousness, is still in the process of being formed). Moreover, Ebla's social status, as a piece of merchandise bought and sold without reference to her own wishes, can be seen, in a more general way, as reflecting the fate of Africa as the plaything of Western powers during the colonial era. And indeed, in the interview Farah replied to the suggested allegoric reading that it would be natural for a Somali reader to interpret Ebla after this fashion, since women are traditionally made to represent the nation in Somali poetry and folktales. He added, however, that he had "clean forgotten" about this area of potential symbolism until reminded of it by Somali readers of the novel,[9] and this implied relegation of national themes to the authorial subconscious and the book's subtexts sounds a salutary warning note.

It is, I suspect, only through a wishful and strenuous effort of the allegoric imagination that the downtrodden but irrepressible Ebla can be translated into a parallel image of the nation groping towards its political independence. Ebla may be appropriate as an image of a colonized, subject people, but the prospective continuation of Somali women's patriarchal repression under independence makes her an ill-suited or at best an ironic symbol of free nationhood. These doubts are borne out by Farah's complex, problematic presentation of Woman as Somalia in the later *Sardines* and *Maps*, a treatment which cautions against the idealistic gendering of independent nations and territories in terms of female archetypes. More immediately, Ebla's notions of "freedom" are of a highly individual and of a peculiarly passive kind which makes them a poor match for their political counterparts. She is a perpetually running figure in the novel, more a fugitive from tyranny than a seeker after liberty or justice, her intelligence of the questioning rather than the questing variety. Her actions are an odd mixture of impulsive bids for freedom and resigned capitulations to captors: after the initial decisive breaking out in the caravan journey to Belet-Wane, she merely drifts from house to house and from town to town, stumbling from one arranged marriage to the next. In spite of the premium she places on free choice, each of her partners is, in one way or another, forced upon her by circumstances beyond her control and she becomes, at times, a hilariously passive and impressionable figure, disclaiming all responsibility for her actions:

> The suggestion to marry Tiffo was Asha's, the one to marry Awill was the widow's, the one to get engaged to an old man in the country (she had even forgotten his name now) was her grandfather's. [...] Never for one single instant did she believe that she was responsible for what she was doing. Others were responsible - God was. (pp. 128, 131)

If this is an image of a fledgling nation embracing its freedom, it is not a very flattering or hopeful one and it fails to strike the right seriousness and consistency of tone. The likelier explanation is that the national theme, like Ebla's resurrection in subsequent novels, was an afterthought, not something systematically projected and closely worked out in the text of the book, and is at best only intermittently relevant. The definition of national identity will feature more visibly in the next novel *A Naked Needle*. In Farah's first book, however, the politics are purely domestic: it is in fact - the adumbrations of independence notwithstanding - the most personal and individually-focused, and the least political, of his novels.

From a Crooked Rib is a limited achievement, slighter in stature and thinner in texture than his major work, but it remains a remarkable first novel. It is a radical, iconoclastic work which uses its artless narrator's sceptical intelligence to interrogate a whole gamut of marital and marriage-related issues, ranging from choice of partner and divorce to polygamy, infidelity and the barbaric practice of female infibulation. In its exposure of the evils of patriarchal power, its elevation of the dignity and status of women, and its targeting of the criminal waste of half the population's potential, the novel contains in embryonic form the vision of much of Farah's mature fiction. As in this later work, both tribalism and Islam are seen to be in negative and reactionary collaboration with the subjugation of women. And, as in the later novels, though in a less tangibly and threateningly political way, the family serves as a microcosm of the world beyond, a world in which Ebla can expect to be controlled, exploited and abused by men, as she is in the domestic context by her grandfather, brother and male cousin. In both spirit and form, however, *From a Crooked Rib* is essentially comic picaresque, a catalogue of Candide-like matrimonial misadventures and sexual nomadism which imparts a quirky humour to even the grimmest features of Somali life. It is also a meticulously observed, detailed and documented work. The light, noise and smell of the African world are keenly and sensuously evoked, and the bizarre mishmash of twentieth century life on the continent - tribal wars and Italian study tours, jet planes and ink-drinking divorce rituals - is exactly rendered. Though they are still some way from fruition, Farah's formidable narrative powers and poetic talents are latently evident in this early work, ready to unfold onto the larger canvasses of the major fiction.

Chapter Three
Couples: *A Naked Needle*

Farah's second novel, *A Naked Needle,* marks a change of pace and style and is a more versatile and experimental performance, with a problematic sense of historical reality. It is set in Mogadiscio during the early days of the Somali Revolution, sometime between Siyad Barre's Soviet-backed military coup of October 1969 and December 1972, when the book was finished. The novel is on first impression a Somali-English love story, albeit of a very peculiar kind and one which is foregrounded against the mixed fortunes of a series of interracial marriages. But it is also a political panorama of the new revolutionary society, complete with satiric portraits of its power-elites, and a stylistic *tour de force* that draws up a mental map of the Somali capital, combining a geographical tour of the city with a summary of the country's postwar history.

As the novel opens its mercurial narrator Koschin, a young Western-educated Somali intellectual, is thrown into a state of panic and confusion by the imminent arrival of his English girlfriend Nancy who has suddenly decided to take up his half-serious offer of marriage if neither of them were to find partners within two years of Koschin's leaving England. His narrative is a meandering mish-mash of personal flashbacks, records of encounters with other racially mixed couples, social comment and current political surveys. These are erratically interspersed with his confused preparations for Nancy's arrival, his eventual reception of her at another couple's flat (he cannot raise the willpower to meet her at the airport), and the city tour which he conducts her on in the novel's fifth "movement." Koshin's present-tense narrative, simultaneous with the events of a single day in his life, is written in the egocentric form of the free-flowing monologue, in which the distinctions between thought and speech are so blurred that it is not always possible to tell whether his tirades are delivered in actuality or in imagination - whether they are addressed to the real Nancy or to the idea or memory of her. His tone throughout is noncommital and inconclusive, his mood drifting and vacillating, continually staving off decision and seeking distraction in political observations.

The narrator's dilemmas are twofold - about his marital status and his political loyalties - and these are interwoven, albeit with limited success, in the course of his monologue. Koschin is at once raconteur and reporter, romantic revolutionary and astute political commentator, idealist and realist, and he subsequently spends a lot of time in the book trying to stoke up his wavering faith in what is clearly a failing revolution. At the time of Nancy's visit he is still determinedly celebrating the "revolutionary" event of the 1969 coup which ended the chaos of colonial parliamentary models: "Before this blessed Revolution, Nancy, there were over sixty political parties in this Country of Curiosity. [...] Each major tribe had a party to its name, each major party had a major tribe to support her."[1] His euphoria, however, is a self-consciously hollow one, maintained as it is only by suppressing his growing awareness of the Supreme Revolutionary Council's betrayal of the Revolution's original ideals of economic independence, sexual equality and detribalization (early in the novel he defiantly ejects an old man who comes to make tribal claims upon his income).

In *A Naked Needle* a number of contradictory currents converge, without quite making contact, in Koschin's permeative revolutionized consciousness and life-style. Though an urbanized intellectual and teacher, he chooses to live in the primitive squalor of a shanty town brothel. He can be both critical and - before the American woman Barbara - defensive of the state's degradation of Somali women. They are "serviles in the society," he tells her. "They like it that way, being Somalis" (p. 68). His progressive public declarations - "Women should be seen and not hurt" - do not quite chime with his private sexual chauvinism: in the past he has beaten Nancy and much of his present narrative is taken up by hysterically misogynistic diatribes against foreign wives. Though he is himself a party to the offence, and perhaps partly because of this, Koschin is preoccupied by the threat to national unity and social fabric posed by the presence of foreigners and infidels, particularly white women, in a devout Muslim society. In this he is profoundly Islamic in attitude: "Do not hold on to your marriages with unbelieving women," runs one verse of the Koran.[2] Although he takes special pride in the government's recent scripting of the Somali language, he knows that Somalia is still an essentially oral society where there are a hundred pharmacies to every bookshop, a higher consumption rate in antibiotics than in intellectual products, and where politics are still conducted by semi-illiterates through oral processes: ominously, there is already a government embargo on books and written information. Most noticably, Koschin is a defiant individualist - "a happy man is one who doesn't let others live his life for him" (p. 143) - who is deeply suspicious of propagandist art, government indoctrination programs and the deification of generals. At odds with this free-spirited individualism, however, is a naive revolutionary idealism that enables him to "turn a dead ear" (the phrase is his own) to evidence of the gathering forces of political repression: the bandaged feet of Bulxan just back from the police cells, his friend Mohamed's razor-cut after a political argument with his barber, and the menacing police car hovering over the last pages of the book, all of which Koschin blithely ignores. The liberal humanist Mohamed, who sounds the first warnings of the "terror and horror from dawn to dusk" being ushered in by KGB-trained revolutionaries, accordingly accuses him of "stinking" from holding ideas in which he does not really believe - an intellectual rot reflected in his poor personal hygiene.

At the same time, Koschin's alert critical eye falls upon instances of national corruption, political betrayals and foreign intrusions that are becoming impossible to ignore. Chief among these are nepotistic appointments to the foreign service, a neocolonial education system with Italian as its medium of instruction, the strengthening Soviet presence, and the Somali elite's flocking to join decadent African intellectuals in United Nations' offices and Western universities to escape the squalor and poverty of the masses. He also singles out the behaviour of the expatriates' home equivalents at the Europeanized Mogadiscio Club:

> The so-called intellectuals of Somalia, the brightest sons and daughters of Puntland, the best that have made home with a degree in their hands, almost all of them, or the ones who count, are at this party, speaking impeccable English or Italian, dropping hot names. Ho Chi Min, Mao Tse Tung; and they are here at this party warming themselves up with wine and women while the age-old poverty, ignorance and idiocy hang over them like shadows. Do they care for the country? With the birth of day, I'm sure they'll have nothing to speak of but the fair ladies they conquered the night before. (p. 135)

Koschin targets political and sexual sell-outs alike, unleashing the same scorn upon incompetent military governments, American wives who undermine the nation's cultural integrity, and Somali males who seek "honorary" whiteness through their sexual conquests, even though the Soviet Embassy, in true imperialist style, penalizes the Russian women who marry them. Through all this he remains painfully aware of the thin line revolutionary Somalia is treading between old and new colonial masters (Britain and Italy, Russia and America) and between the Western and Eastern power-blocs: "Whoever will do any good for this country and for Africa, I shall back till I die. [...] If these fail to do that they owe us, I shall declare war against them, single-handed even though I am" (p. 152). These declarations of war are, of course, empty rhetorical gestures destined to have no effect upon their targets. Koschin will not be given the opportunity to vote the failed military regime out of power and such regimes are partly the responsibility of educated men like himself who gave them support and credibility in the first place. Koschin, as D. R. Ewen wrily observes, is the kind of intellectual who "wages and wins wars by staying out of them,"[3] and the only positive action he performs in the novel is to resign from his teaching job.

And yet the very element of unreality or insubstantiality given expression in Koschin's tokenism is, perhaps, not fortuitous but may, on the contrary, be a key ingredient of the style and mode of Farah's novel, in which the illusion of historical reality is sustained only up to a certain point. *A Naked Needle* is the most openly, if inexpertly, "postmodern" of Farah's fictions. The book both is and is not about the historical actuality of post-revolution Somalia at which it is obtusely angled, and its "truth to reality" is problematized at the outset by the disclaimer's enigmatic warning that there are "no real characters where none is intended" and "no true incident where none is mentioned" (which raises the questions of what, exactly, are "real" characters and "true" incidents). Farah's Mogadiscio, as presented by his wayward guide, is a jumble of languages and cultures, ethnic quarters and ghettos, and of migrating embassy officials, foreign experts and Italianized intellectuals with English girlfriends, American wives and Russian mistresses in tow. Even in its "straight" realistic representation, it is a patchwork product of the colonial imagination and a post-colonial variant of those zoned postwar European cities that feature in American postmodern fiction (Pynchon, Hawkes, Vonnegut), in which the locales traversed are so diverse and disparate that they seem to belong (and often do) to different worlds. Only here the difference is that reality is zoned into the surreal extremes of obscene wealth and destitution, the Western-colonial and the primitive-indigenous. The city, like so many African cities, is an unreal place, an unnatural colonial imposition that peters out into rusty shanty towns of hovels and open drains where native Africa exists permanently "on the periphery of starvation" (p. 113). The opulent boulevards lined with concrete monoliths run out into rubble, the few miles of tarred roads into sand. As if to compound the very arbitrariness and nightmare quality of the colonial "fiction", Koschin undertakes the further reimagining of the city and its post-colonial African context by the tried postmodernist technique of displacing and deranging customary historical and geographical associations. Written at a slight angle to history, Koschin's narrative mischievously piles misquotation upon misinformation and mixes invented anecdotes with recorded ones, so that the facts are given to us more than a little askew. It has been observed, for example, that Bakhtu-Rida secondary school in Khartoum where Koschin claims to have been schooled is not a secondary school and is not in Khartoum,[4] while the real Fanon's death was from leukemia, perhaps less romantic than the cigar-toting guerrilla's death from lung cancer which is substituted for it here.

Furthermore, each of the book's racially mixed relationships is passed as a matter of course through the postmodernist fiction's deconstructive sieve of stock literary types and tropes, reduced by time and over familiarity to comic-strip level (here, the Dark Lady, the Colonial Mistress, the White Destroyer), with the effect that the symbolic or representative signifier is given priority over its referent: "I don't like what you *represent*," Koschin tells the American woman Barbara (p. 145). Koschin, meanwhile, devises for Nancy an unashamedly novelettish past full of grandfathers and fiances martyred in the noble struggles of romantic Latin American insurrections, mixing historical anecdotes with imagined ones and revolutionary romances (Nancy's supposed ancestry) with "real" ones (her present). Subsequently, it is left unclear whether or not these magazine-romance revolutions are to be seen as existing in the same world as, and being of the same status and order of experience as, the historical Somali revolution which she now finds herself in the midst of. Are they the stuff of stories previously narrated by her to him and now relayed, with additions, to the reader, or are they the wild concoctions of Koschin's exuberant imagination, or simply constituents of the author's single, all-embracing literary fabulation? Third world reality has been so remodelled by the free play of the narrative signifier that the two revolutions come to coexist in an impossible space which exists nowhere except in the projected fictional universe of the written text. What kind of narrative needle is Farah/Koschin using to stitch together the different orders of reality zoned in his novel?

Koschin expresses the wish not to be the needle of the novel's title and epigraph, the needle that "clothes others whilst it remains naked" (p. 70) and so appears to resist a number of implied aesthetic options. These include, from the illusionist mode of modern realism to which the novel only partly subscribes, the "mind erosion" of the Flaubertian artist who denudes himself of material for his art, which he himself therefore remains radically unlike, staying "naturally leafless, naked during all seasons and at all times, while on other trees flowers are conceived and blossom" (p. 70). But the options also include the classical Joycean artist, aesthetically and linguistically self-absorbed, uninvolved in and unaffected by what he creates, and the postmodern threader of anti-illusionist or pseudo-illusionist constructs in which he does not believe. Of course, Farah does not wish to belong to any of these groups of writers and even if we allow for the novel's verbal pyrotechnics - the virtuoso alliteration, graphic onomatopoeia and outlandish homonymic punning - his committed stance is as far removed as is imaginable from Joyce's neutralized aestheticism. But the book's very unsureness of what kind of novel it might be may be the surest indicator of the kind of novel it really is. It bears, in fact, many of the hallmarks of the postmodernist metafiction, notably its self-preoccupied textuality (the incestuous literary allusions and interior word games), and its narrative reflexiveness. Nancy is described on the second page as "an epilogue that spoils the strong point of a novel", the book contains at least one reference to its own publisher and the series in which it appeared, and Koschin, whose friend reads *Finnegan's Wake* as a "nightcap," confesses to have written a thesis on Joyce: this habit of incorporating a character's written work into the author's is repeated with Margaritta's thesis on African National Security Services in *Sweet and Sour Milk*, Medina's critique of the revolution in *Sardines*, and Askar's court defence on the last page of *Maps*, which refers us back to the novel we have just read. The hard distinctions between modes of fictional discourse are blurred by the Joycean amalgam of interior monologue and conversational fragments, and the lines between fictional and other modes of discourse by the virtuoso stylistics and wordplay and the metafictional reflexiveness.

Needle is additionally unusual among Farah's novels insofar as it is about couples, not families, and Koschin's playful, parodic manipulation of the types and tropes of race and sex in the context of mixed marriages and engagements - tropes that are by turns challenged and upheld - also needs to be seen in terms of the book's problematic narrative mode and with reference to narrative needles that may *un*stitch and pull things apart. In this novel the human reality of the female interlocutor, ominously surnamed Stonegrave, has to fight its way through a dense narrative fog of stock literary figures and stereotypes, spread by her intended before she appears. Nancy, whom Koschin has inexplicably "always associated with death," becomes, in rapid succession, a shadow and ghost, "a human deformity, the white person, [...] a ghost of the living dead" (p. 113), La Belle Dame sans Merci, the Dark Lady, the deathly white mistress given to the pathological clutching of crucifixes and recitation of medieval hymns during love-making, and much more of the same kind. The writing in these passages has a precious, self-parodying and self-debunking literariness which seems deliberately to disable belief and which culminates in Nancy's hysterically overstated introduction: "She offers him a love that has decayed inside her heart. [...] Dressed in a black nylon two-piece dress, and a dark jumper, and dark shoes: and this, a pact with the darkness of death, my God!" (p. 78). Once the Gothic trappings have been removed, what emerges from the caricature is the female sexual archetype of the colonial mistress, the white dominator and destroyer. By bringing the real Nancy's gentle, patient nature to bear upon this model that he has prepared for her, Koschin, like Fanon before him, then proceeds to attempt a "contractual marriage [...] between the image he hated and the woman he cared for" in order to "crush out of existence an image of the dominator" (p. 134).

This latter image rampages through most of Koschin's speculations about interracial sexual relations, particularly his fantastic projections from the Mildred-Barre marriage shortly before Nancy's arrival:

> Nietzsche said never wed a woman without her whip. Ask for the whip before the hand. [...] Never buy a Nigger without a stick to beat him with.
>
> And this poor fellow from the land of the pagans, green in his hand-me-down suit, falls for an American dream of a woman, and licks the ground she walks on. [...] And this pagan chooses to prostrate himself before the the American dream of a woman, what boobs, what a figure, what a mouth to to kiss, he chooses to flatten himself on the tiled floor, he argues, because he needs her, and she chooses never to pick him up, never to offer him a helping hand. [...] The man straight from the land of jungles, he continued sinking down more and more, never denying her the rights of a deity, until he had been reduced to a bare physique with no mind.
>
> What are we after, the so-called intelligentsia of this country, running like Paris after those foreign women, sluts of a kind, in their own countries, despised here in ours - what are we after? Is it what Fanon says we are after? Or something below that? [...] Why are we unsatisfied with our own? (pp. 31, 33, 42)

Of course, Koschin protests too much. His too glib espousal of the stereotype, whether genuine or ironic, is clearly meant to be taken as an index to his own immature, almost paranoid, anxiety over Nancy's visit and is sustained only by misquotation and misrepresentation. Nietzsche's famous quip about the whip is inverted - "never wed a woman without *her* whip" - to promote the stale sado-masochistic colonial paradigm of white female power-lust and black male prostration; and thence the Fanonian model, treated in *Black Skin, White Masks*, of the white mistress and the black love-slave who, in a white society, desires only to be loved as if white.[5] A few minutes later Koschin is ready to admit his blunder in his assessment of the Mildred-Barre marriage: the latter, as his own interrogation of Barre reveals, in fact reverses the Fanonian model. Here the white woman is not the victimizer but, lured by lies of wealth and tribal hospitality, is the duped, trapped victim for whom the husband impossibly seeks acceptance as an "honorary" Somali in a culturally alien society. The black man does not, in this case, want to be loved as "white," by the white woman in her white society; he wants *her* to be loved as a Somali in a Muslim one. Most of the unhappiness in this marriage is hers, and it is chiefly his doing. Stereotypically, Barre blames the nuclearization of the extended Somali family upon the foreign wife - "They make you cut off your ties with your brothers and sisters, they insinuate the idea from the moment they set their feet here that you must live your own life with them" (p. 28) - but in fact the opposite is true. Barre beats his wife, exposes her to the rigid customs and codes of an alien clan culture, and, finally, by abandoning her to its suffocating intimacies and boredom, drives her to a suicide attempt. Farah tentatively offers, as an alternative to the cultural collisions of the Mildred-Barre marriage, the more realistic compromise, albeit with built-in infidelities, achieved by the American Barbara and the Western-oriented Mohamed, a Somali who has already "detribalized" himself. "I have adjusted totally, I should say, to the conditions that are prevalent here, conditions that may put off any woman from anywhere else in the world," Barbara claims, offering herself as the model of cultural compromise. The claim rings hollow, however, when she reveals that her knowledge of her husband's language extends only to "the basic Somali words for communication" and adds the qualifier, "But it is only him [Mohamed] that I must get used to, not a whole tribe, if you see what I mean" (pp. 62, 64). Moreover, when Barre discloses to Koschin that Barbara turned to himself for sexual satisfaction within a month of the birth of her daughter and during Mohamed's brief absence, the American woman's abject failure to observe or to understand Islamic conventions becomes glaringly evident. Subsequently, it transpires that, whatever happiness Mohamed and Barbara have found in their flexible relationship, it has been achieved by his shift towards Western behaviour patterns rather than by any accommodation of Somali traditions and values on her part (we hear in the later novel *Sardines* that Barbara is living in Rome, revelling in her new freedom, and assume that the marriage has failed).

Whatever the relative merits of these two relationships, it becomes clear in the first half of the novel, in any case, that race and colour are not the real issues at stake but religion and the devout Muslim code on women: thus Koschin foresees that Nancy's Western Catholicism, not her whiteness, will be the main source of Somali hostility. Farah constantly complicates racial polarities with other factors and the effect of his playing off of figure against fact, image against particular instance, is to set up Fanonian stereotypes - figures ripe for demolition - only to undermine and dismantle them. Significantly, the racially mixed marital and sexual relationships treated in the first four "movements" of the narrative are neither developed as vehicles for broader political statements (for example, about subtle new forms of Russian and American neo-imperialism) nor declared exempt from and therefore irrelevant to political realities: they are simply dropped. Farah is finally not interested in the extent to which black-white sexual relations reflect, or are distinguishable from, patterns of African powerlessness and Western domination (in this respect the novel is a world away from the politico-sexual polemics of a book like Ayi Kwei Armah's *Why Are We So Blest?*). Not surprisingly, the perfunctory interweaving of foreign political and sexual incursions into Somali life does not proceed beyond the fourth movement.

A Naked Needle has been called "an intellectual novel" and Farah described Koschin in an interview as "a man whose only function is to think," but added that "he finds himself in an ideologically confused country" and, consequently, is himself confused.[6] Whatever the source of the narrator's mental confusion, two things are clear about his supposed "thinking." Firstly, it includes a great deal of axiomatic non-think: "American women are a thorn in the flesh," "Theft has no quantity." Secondly, he is much given, in his free-wheeling intellectual fulminations, to the exuberant tossing around of archetypes and tropes from the world's literatures and philosophies - tropes which exist in contradistinction with whatever substantial human reality is realized in the novel. In particular, the Fanonian stereotypes are, deliberately and grotesquely, unequal to "reality," as constructed in the illusionist mode, and, insofar as they fail to develop the book's cross-racial sexual relationships as valid vehicles for social and political comment, they are *de*constructed by them. Once the geographical and historical tour of the city, in movements Five and Six, is underway and the narrative starts to splinter into a discrete succession of personal encounters and exchanges, the novel's sexual centre of interest is virtually dissolved.

It resurfaces briefly amid the political *longeurs* of the last long movement at the Club in the cliched cameo of Mahed and his graceless Russian mistress, whom Koschin dubs "a thing of laughter for a wife" (p. 167). Here, at least, Fanon's model holds up: for some of the new Soviet-trained power *arrivistes*, any white woman will do. Finally, the sexual interest reemerges briefly at the return of Nancy in the last five pages. The lovers bed down in Koschin's hovel, to which Nancy, symbolically, is led blind into the dark, though they do so "without ever raising the issue between them," and this leaves some uncertainty about whether their relationship is the novel's main issue or even an issue at all. It is, moreover, not clear why Koschin's aloof, defensive reserve suddenly capitulates to Nancy's tenderness at the end and why, after being irritated by her for most of the day, he apparently comes to accept her and believes them to have achieved mutual understanding through honesty (a process not demonstrated).

It has been Koschin's exasperating habit throughout his monologue, and it is finally the novel's, to touch upon topics that cannot or are not intended to be carried through. The eventual outcome of these narrative vagaries is the unhooking of the private relationship from the political commentary and of the psychological from the historical interest, during which process the flat "literary" representations - the types and archetypes - come away from the more "realistic" ones. Needles, of course, unstitch as well as stitch and, whether by default or by design, the narrative finally pulls itself apart and falls into two separate halves. This is not the book's only weakness. Koschin's invective is too indiscriminate and unfocused to have much impact and is really the random flailing of a disappointed idealist, a man who cannot accept his own political disillusionment and continues to rail at everything that does not live up to his wilting revolutionary dreams. Thus, fitful critiques of neocolonialism and tribalism, government philistinism and corruption, foreign wives and imperial agents, are all amorphously jumbled together in his tirade and mixed in with more deeply felt personal laments for the plight of a native Africa that lives eternally on the margins of existence. Farah, it should be remembered, was still only 27 when he completed *Needle* (in 1972, though publication was delayed until 1976 out of fear for the author's safety), and it is essentially the *jeu d'esprit* of a young writer who has not yet reached the peak of his powers. In the next novel we hear that Koschin has been arrested and reduced to a vegetable in a state mental asylum. In retrospect, the attempt to present the political tumult of a nation in the throes of revolution through his personal breakdown seems, despite the energy of the writing, to have been a bold but flawed experiment, limited in possibility, and it is no surprise that it was not repeated.

Today the book remains something of an oddity in Farah's fiction, seeming not quite to belong to the main body of his work, and remains of interest principally on two counts. Firstly, there is the complex of contradictory attitudes towards the Somali Revolution which converge in the narrative consciousness, and the concomitant puzzle of the author's own moral position at the time of writing. Happily, Farah's fair-minded openness to experience combines with Koschin's histrionics to debunk each of the stale race-sex archetypes thrown up by the unstable narrator's imagination. Yet everything is not plain accord, or discord, between author and character. *Needle* is the only one of Farah's books to take anything like a benevolent view of the dictator and also, significantly perhaps, the only one that he has not been keen to have reprinted. Here Siyad Barre, henceforth "the General," is merely the "Old Man"; he is "decent, honest" and "wishes to do something for the country"; and reponsibility for his deification is naively attributed to his underlings and the populace (p. 80). At the same time, Koschin's admiration for his achievements is guarded and at times jeeringly ironic. He notes also the gross maladministration and venality; the neocolonial connivance with Catholic mission profiteering, the use of Italian workmen in preference to the Somali unemployed; the poorly trained teachers and the dearth of school laboratories; and the starving nomads who still die with their cattle. Koschin's vacillations, it seem, serve as a barometer to the young author's own uncertainties and anxieties. Farah, by turns, identifies himself with and dissociates himself from Koschin's viewpoint and in his indecisive moments appears, impossibly, to attempt both at once, using the tricks of the metafiction to simultaneously affirm and deny his narrator's authentic reality. Thus to some extent the novel is implicated in - indeed, is a party to and succumbs to - its protagonist's intellectual and ideological confusion.

The second main area of interest is Koschin's position in relation to Somali oral tradition. For all his pride in the revolutionary government's recent scripting of the Somali language, Koschin is at heart a garrulously oral creature, given to torrents of talk and intoxicated with the sheer sound of words. Hence the pure joy in eruptions of verbal wit and the frantic alliterative couplings and echoing assonances: "And they quite quietly consume their consomme," "we tire our human tyres" (pp. 77, 92). He is, moreover, a fount of oral folklore - he uses the local fable of the frog outwitting the fox to characterize Somalia's relations with its intellectuals (p. 160) - and he thinks to a surprising extent in proverbs and platitudes drawn from the oral idiom. Koschin, the urban intellectual, comes originally (though he has come a long way from it) from the same illiterate bookless culture as the peasant girl Ebla. He hails from a society whose oral modes of communication are about to be menaced by the strengthening dictatorship of the General and which are seen here for the last time in their pristine healthy condition prior to their political perversion and exploitation. Nevertheless, he sees, correctly, that the oral code still has a kind of currency and hegemony even in the new society. "There is no government-fixed price, neither do you get a receipt," he remarks ominously, "all is done orally, we are an oral society, and one has to trust [the vendor]" (p. 111). But the vendor in the new political order is the government. The price-fixer is an increasingly despotic military regime which, if the truth be admitted, actually lives in terror of the written word and which, in the grim trilogy of novels that follows, will ruthlessly employ oral-based techniques of surveillance and repression to "short-change" the people. Koschin therefore, in his rapturous enthusiasm for the new orthography, is an unwitting accomplice to the political hypocrisy of the new literacy, an unsuspecting collaborator with the coming terror to which he will fall victim.

CHAPTER FOUR
Fathers and Sons: *Sweet and Sour Milk*

After the surface glitter, off-handed stylistic brilliance and sometimes flippant tone of *A Naked Needle*, the next book is sombre stuff, befitting the gravity of the worsening Somali political situation, and the trilogy it launches is Farah's most artistically mature and intellectually complex work to date.[1] The failure of revolutionary rhetoric to match reality in the previous book pales beside the daily dawn disappearances, the secret interrogations with torture and mass executions under the totalitarian dictatorship which the Somali revolution has drifted into in the five or so years that have passed. Somalis now live in terror of the loitering police-informer, the midnight knock on the door. Koschin himself has been interned, either in prison or in a mental asylum where he is being reduced to a vegetative state: as with everything else in this book, the information is not clear. At least, in the last book, the antics of the Supreme Revolutionary Council still made some kind of sense. In *Sweet and Sour Milk*, however, we are in a demented, deranged world; an Orwellian nightmare of unpersons and rearranged history in which terror and unreason have taken up an autonomous existence, moving in an orbit of their own and rivalled only by the surrealist poetics which Farah devises to deal with them.

In the Prologue to the novel Soyaan Keynaan, economic adviser to the President, dies, apparently poisoned at a dinner with a government minister at the house of his father's second wife. By falsifying the facts of his life and his last words - Soyaan is officially reported as having said, farcically, "Labour is honour and there is no General but our General"[2] - the regime then immediately proceeds to turn the dead man into a revolutionary hero, an undertaking which his father Keynaan, ex-policeman and now informer to the dictatorship, is only too happy to collaborate with. Soyaan's twin brother Loyaan, a country dentist who has no experience of the labyrinthine passages of political life, embarks upon a reconstruction of the events of Soyaan's last weeks. Coded messages in his brother's diary soon lead him to a copy of a seditious Memorandum hidden in Soyaan's clothes, a document enquired after by a government minister at the funeral. Further evidence is scrambled together from Soyaan's mistress Margaritta, by whom he has a young son called Marco, and from his friend Ibrahim, and his doctor, the suspicious Ahmed-Wellie, and a pattern begins to emerge: it becomes apparent that the dead man had become a leading figure in subversive, anti-Soviet activities and was murdered, with the aid of a Russian doctor, as part of a government plot. Soyaan's suspected poisoning is impossible to prove because his father, on instructions from the regime, invokes Islamic tradition to refuse a post-mortem as sacrilegious. Furthermore, in the atmosphere of fear and suspicion sown by the dictator, Loyaan is unable to trust the testimony of any of Soyaan's confederates and confidantes: the Italian-Somali "mistione" Margaritta is also an ex-mistress of the Minister of Police; Ahmed-Wellie and Ibrahim insinuate that they are fellow conspirators but the former appears to be a government spy, despite his later arrest, and suspicion is cast on the latter by his friendship with the suspicious doctor; and the interrogation and torture of Mulki, the typist who allegedly prepared Soyaan's Memorandum and whom Loyaan never gets to meet, is shrouded in mystery. After a futile interrogative assault on the minister who was present at Soyaan's last meal and a brief spell of detention, Loyaan's lone quest for the truth peters out inconclusively with the government's decision to pack him off to Belgrade as a "diplomat" in the Soviet embassy. The exact motive and manner of Soyaan's death and the reliability of a subversive "Group of Ten" formed around him remain uncertain. As Loyaan awaits his departure, the novel ends with an ominous, ambiguous knock on the door.[3]

It becomes clear in this narrative of political manoeuvrings and intrigues that Farah does not, like some African writers, conceive the traditional past, its values and forms of expression, as unsullied alternatives and possible modes of counter-discourse to the political corruptions, tyrannies and neo-imperial intrusions of the post-colonial era. Rather, the traditional forms are implicated in the new terror, for the new military despotism is revealed to be but the patriarchal authoritarianism of the Somali family writ large, and the General is seen to answer to, and to represent something authentic in, Somali life. In the following trilogy of novels, in which the focus of Farah's fiction switches from the unit of the individual relationship to that of the family, the collusions of family and state authoritarianisms, and of domestic and political patriarchy, are commonplace phenomena.

The family is of first importance throughout the sinister political proceedings of *Sweet and Sour Milk*, which plunges the reader into the tangled network of patriarchal and polygamous kinship structures in a country ruled by a tribal oligarchy. Professing all the while to be governed by the principles of "scientific socialism," this oligarchy in fact dispenses power, nepotistically, through the polygamous family network to the dictator's cousins and kinsmen, excluding all who are not of his clan. The medium of political persuasion and control is the family unit, the enforcing agent the patriarchal father, and the set-up is given its most naked expression in two instances of Keynaan's brutality: he beats his pregnant second wife, Beydan, for insulting the Minister of Police and his first wife, Qumman, for daring to suggest that their son did not die of natural causes (Qumman is right about the crime but has the wrong culprit, blaming Beydan for Soyaan's poisoning). The manipulative political pressures on the family are present, however, at a more general and pervasive level throughout the novel. The houses of civil servants are numbered by the Security police; their families are registered with political "Orientation Centres" to which they must report thrice-weekly, and it is for the sake of these families that the bureaucratic breadwinners acquiesce to the regime and give their assent to its lies:

> To stay on, you break and praise. You do this in order to eke out an indecent living for the weaker members of the family, for mother, for sister and for the children. If you don't do this, you end up in prison. [...] there are the bureaucrats who have no political ambitions nor social awareness but who reason thus: 'I have a wife and children. It is for their sake I serve this regime in order that I have a means of earning a living; it is for their sake that I prostrate myself, that I accept to be humiliated. (pp. 74, 107)

The oral network of "Dionysius's Ear" uncovered in Soyaan's Memorandum - a corps of illiterate informers reporting rumour and hearsay to the regime - has a similarly insidious domestic base. Ibrahim explains that the "ears" planted by the security system "sprout in every homestead": in the absence of trade unions and other organized protest groups, informers are pressed from the family by threats to the safety of its members. It is for the survival and security of the family that the mother Qumman gratefully accepts the "posthumous honour" conferred by the regime upon her son and its accompanying "lucrative gratuity" ("a dead man is less useful than his shoes," runs a Somali proverb). It is with a view to the preservation of the family that the women in the novel counsel caution and compromise, tempering the defiant but often futile idealism of their men with a common-sense pragmatism: "Soyaan is dead. And you are not. So please," Ladan exhorts Loyaan (p. 101). And it is, finally, in the name of the family that Keynaan connives at the posthumous misrepresentation of his son, thus ensuring his own professional rehabilitation, his promotion to a lieutenancy and the restoration of a security-providing income.

It is subsequently not surprising, given the centrality of the family in the life of the nation, that it becomes a microcosm of the state, the domestic situation closely entwined with the political one. Thus when Keynaan embarrasses the regime with his excessive zeal by torturing to death one of its victims and a political scapegoat is required to avert a tribal mutiny, he is not only removed from his office but is forced to marry the victim's widow (Beydan), so that his domestic life becomes an extension of his professional one. And when the General hypocritically hijacks the traditional purification rite of the Rendezvous of the Brooms to clean the city for a visit by foreign dignitaries, the public ceremonial performance of the women is merely an enlargement of their private domestic chores. Here, men are represented by their mothers, sisters and housemaids:

> Ladan and Qumman had changed into their work clothes. They would go there, sweep and clean, they would prepare the village's roads just as a mother would a daughter on the day of marriage [...] Women formed the majority of those present here, for they left their husbands and brothers to take a siesta after the day's school, office or whatever. "It is very untraditional to see a man with broom in hand." [...] Women as saviours, women as protectors; women as the backbone of the family's unity and safety. (pp. 186, 190-91)

At a loss to explain why these women, on whom Somali men are completely dependent, allow themselves to be treated so badly by them, Loyaan instinctively analogizes inter-familial relations with political oppression: "There is mutual need: a torturer needs somebody who is willing to be tortured, no?" (p. 190).

Indeed, Farah's novel devotes so much attention to the workings of families because of the overlapping needs which bind domestic and national politics together, making them interdependent and mutually supportive. He reveals that, for all the vaunted egalitarianism of Somalia's traditional political institutions, the authoritarian family structure at the roots of the society actually conditions people to and predisposes them towards the tyranny officially endorsed and institutionalized by military regimes. These submissive attitudes arise from the intrinsic nature of Somali life: they are imbibed with the mother's milk (by turns sweet and sour) and, as is shown by Loyaan's traumatic childhood memories of his father's terrifying brutality, they continue into adulthood. As a result, the twin repressive institutions of family and state are able to invoke each other's authority and sanction each other's violence, and this inter-reliance is made explicit by the epigraphic use of a quotation from Wilhelm Reich: "In the figure of the father the authoritarian state has its representative in every family, so that the family becomes its most important instrument of power" (p. 97).

After Farah's usual fair-minded fashion, the patriarchal dragons, and the matriarchal ones of the next book, are allowed to have their say: "You have no common ideology and no principles," Keynaan tells Loyaan. "You work for the interests of the countries in which you received your academic training" (p. 93). There is at least some truth in the first part of this statement: the new generation of dissidents which looks to Western liberal humanism for its inspiration has little of its own to put in the place of the coherent tribal heritage which the Soviet-backed ideologues are careful to keep intact and to appropriate for their own uses. Nevertheless, Farah is unrelenting in his pinpointing of patriarchal bigotry as the principal source of current political authoritarianism, religious hypocrisy and police-state terrorism. Keynaan declares himself to Loyaan:

> I am the father. It is my prerogative to give life and death as I find fit. I've chosen to breathe life into Soyaan. And remember one thing, Loyaan: if I decide this minute to cut you in two, I can. The law of this land invests in men of my age the power. I am the Grand Patriarch. (p. 95)

Thus the father turns himself into the household replica and representative of the dictator, and this features in his behaviour in a number of ways. Like the General, he takes refuge in religious obscurantism ("Only Allah knows, only Allah") and he misuses the Koran to deny equality to men and to marginalize women as "inferior beings," fit only for sex, childbearing and menial work, and to cow them into submission (the General's execution of the rebel sheikhs and Keynaan's inheritance, against her will, of the widow of a deceased kinsman are, in fact, both highly *un*Koranic). Both men are uneducated and semi-illiterate: the General is incapable of reading long documents and Keynaan, who still thinks that the world is flat, bursts his sons' ball because they have drawn a mini-atlas on it. And in each case this ignorance is invested with power - most disturbingly, the god-like power to "breathe life" into false, invented versions of reality. "Heroes are *made*," Loyaan reminds the Minister to the Presidency. "Every nation needs heroes in which to invest a past" (p. 183). Keynaan simply follows the orders and example of the master-manufacturer, the General. "I breathe life into his [Soyaan's] name. I make him honourable," he casuistically defends himself against his son's accusations. "You hold me responsible for his death. I believe I am responsible for the spiritual revival of his name" (p. 95). At Loyaan's arrest the police official threatens him with a line from the Koran - "God takes the breath He lends to one" (p. 201) - which simultaneously takes in the deity, the deified General and the patriarchal father. In each case, the god-figure's supreme authority is not limited to the power of life and death over his subjects but extends beyond death to control of the deceased's reputation: "Legally it was within the male parent's absolute prerogative to act on behalf of a dead son or daughter or wife" (p. 86). Finally, although Keynaan does not encourage the jealous rivalries of his wives, these help to maintain his rule in much the same way as the General's division of the clans.

At the material level Keynaan is, of course, closely linked by his official dealings and tribal kinship with the nation's prime political patriarchs, the General and the Minister to the Presidency, and he becomes, effectively, the domestic arm of the regime's security system. He combines the roles of ex-torturer and paid informer to the regime with that of terrorizer of his wives and children: in return for the former services, the state upholds his patriarchal rights and guarantees support for his abuse of parental power, against which his family has no right of appeal. Keynaan conspires with the defamation of his son, harmlessly dissolving Soyaan's secret subversive activities by allowing him to become posthumously a property of the state, a "loyal" follower of the General and "*son* of the revolution." The father makes the state, by proxy, the guardian of his son's posterity, transferring to it his traditional rights of parental control and, as we have seen, counting upon his wives and daughters to accept the posthumous "honour" in the name of the highest of Islamic virtues, the protection and preservation of the family. Thus the embodiment of political and paternal tyranny in the same person makes for the efficient stamping out of subversion, simultaneously, at both public and private, state and familial levels. Along this patriarchal continuum, sexual power is seen as another extension and manifestation of political power. Somalia is a country where a widow is forced by the government to marry the policeman who has murdered her husband, and where a woman (Amina in the next book) is pressed hard to marry one of the political dissidents who has raped her. In *Sweet and Sour Milk* power is imaged as a captive mistress who is pandered to, courted and finally seized by the General, and village brides are offered up to the sadistic whims of visiting African dictators like Amin: "Come: take this key, the symbol of power, and open the clean and shaven legs of our womanhood. Come: take this sceptre, use it as the whip for the sado-masochistic rite to which you've been honourably invited" (p. 186). The Minister of Police, unwrapping a cigar, "broke its polythene with the same cruelty as a rapist would deflower a virgin" (p. 180).

It is in the figure of Keynaan that the most destructive features of the General's regime, and the anger directed at it by the novelist, are focalized. Farah makes it clear that Keynaan is part of a chain of oppression in which he passes on the regime's violence to his family, beating his wives and children when he is humiliated by superior officers at work. But, though this explains him, it does not excuse him. Indeed, there is little to redeem Keynaan, who is a worthless, wretched creature and a criminally irresponsible father for most of the book. He beats his first wife in the hour of their son's death, his second on the eve of her parturition. When the dying Soyaan lists the General's praise-names sung by Dulman on the radio - "The father of the nation. The carrier of wisdom. The provider of comforts" (p. 15) - we observe that the family father is none of these. Far from being a provider, Keynaan is a profligate who squanders the money given him by Soyaan for the upkeep of Beydan on reckless philanderings with girls as young as, and younger than, his own daughter; meanwhile, his first wife Qumman longs for the day when her sons will provide the security that will end her dependence on him. Qumman notes that "fathers are secondary" in the lives of their children but Keynaan does not even merit secondary ranking in his family. He is hated by his sons, who still nurse boyhood fantasies about combining their anger and weaponry to kill him, and he has no place in the prayers or affections of his daughter. A cartoon-creature himself, he shamelessly helps to fabricate a political cartoon for his son to live posthumously on in, selling Soyaan's honour for financial security. By the end of the book he has become a monstrous parasitical growth upon his family, feeding on the ones he is supposed to protect. Keynaan is, in Ibrahim's phrase, "worse than evil," and Loyaan's momentary gesture of reconciliation with him on the penultimate page of the novel is less than convincing.

Thus, family and state, patriarchy and power, are Farah's twin concerns in this novel. The traditional paterfamilias is the primary model for the head of state whose powers, like his own, rest on tribal consent. At a more abstract level, the father, who is the author of and authority over his offspring, is paralleled by the father of the nation who authorizes the mode of reality in which his people live, telling them what they shall believe and deem authentic. "Tell" is the operative word here, for in the General's Somalia the command is an oral, not a written one: the omnipotent, god-like dictator symbolically breathes life into, and takes it away from, his children through the power of the spoken word which has ultimate authority over them. At this point the politics of patriarchy touch importantly upon the oral tradition.

Though he has described Somalia as "a society coming out of the oral tradition into a written form,"[4] Farah has insisted that "you cannot divorce the oral and the literary from one another."[5] These continuities notwithstanding, his fiction has been slower than that of some of his contemporaries - notably Ngugi wa Thiong'o and Ayi Kwei Armah - to recognize the positive strengths and reconstructive potential of traditional cultural values and their oral modes of expression. Farah seeks neither to rehabilitate traditional forms, like Armah in his experimentation with simulated orality in *Two Thousand Seasons* or Ngugi in *Matigari*, nor to discredit and repudiate them, like Yambo Ouologuem in his satiric rendition of griotature in *Bound to Violence*. Rather, he is concerned to show how indigenous traditions, oral as well as domestic, have themselves been implicated in the new political tribulations and terrors of the independent state. Farah has also described the Somalis as a people "moving straight from the oral tradition in the African sense to the oral tradition in the technological sense (television and radio) without going through that middle stage of the written word."[6] This process acquires sinister implications, and the oral tradition its darkest dimensions, in *Sweet and Sour Milk*, where the oral culture is effectively allied with the reactionary forces of tribal authoritarianism and obscurantism. In this novel there is engineered a near-absolute polarization of oral despotism and written revolution, of unalphabeted tyranny and textual subversion, the first category represented by the fathers and the second by the sons. It was Koschin, in the previous novel, who sounded the first warning note about the dangers of excessive reliance on the oral code's modes of communication: "There is no government-fixed price [...] we are an oral society, and one has to trust."[7] The General knows as well as Koschin, and Dulman in the next book, that Somali hearts are won through their ears: his regime's repressive surveillance techniques thrive on oral exchanges and are steeped in the existing oral traditions of a still largely illiterate society. The debasement of the oral code by the new political fathers of the nation, and their exploitation of its negative and destructive potential, is one of Farah's principal concerns in the first novel of his *Dictatorship* trilogy.

In the Somalia of *Sweet and Sour Milk* power is still largely oral-based. By the surveillance system of "Dionysius's Ear" - named after the Syracusan tyrant who built a cave in the shape of a human ear to echo to him his prisoners' whisperings - a barely literate General recruits his security corps of spies and informers from illiterates working entirely in the oral medium and reporting verbally everything they hear. Under the "ear-service" of tyranny, little or nothing is written down: death-certificates are withheld, executed political opponents are buried anonymously in unnumbered graves, and there are no lists of detainees or arrest warrants (phoned instructions suffice), and no written reports and particulars. "No writing-pad, no pen," Loyaan notes of the heavy-booted official who hauls him briefly into detention. "He had not come to take Loyaan's particulars. [...] No minutes would show how long he had been kept here [...] he might be here for six months, a name untraceable, a person unregistered, a man inexistent" (p. 196). The Soviet sponsors of the regime, though they themselves keep thick files on members of the Somali government, take care to preserve the indigenous oral structure as it suits their own political purposes. Under the new Russian-trained Minister to the Presidency, the files on both Somali prisoners and Soviet agents grow progressively thinner until they are eventually invisible. Indeed, there is an embargo on books and written information and the few files that continue to exist can, like Soyaan's, be confiscated for purposes of rewording "history." Texts like his Memorandum and his "Clowns" piece (which apparently had a real underground circulation in a Somali translation)[8] are automatically deemed subversive and are ruthlessly hunted down, with dire results for those found in possession: Ladan discovers in the pockets of Soyaan's trousers details of a new decree that imposes the death penalty for disseminating or exporting printed matter of this kind. "In this country, rumour rules," Margaritta tells him, and it is rumour rather than information that is published:

> The politics of mystification rendered rumours credible. Nothing was ever confirmed. [...] No information was released until a rumour had been published, and nothing was made official until the General's informants had reported back the mood, the feeling of the general public. (p. 196)

In *Sweet and Sour Milk* Farah tackles teasing philosophical questions about the nature of perception and identity in a floating oral reality which mirrors the country's political malaise; a mode of reality in which truth is as indeterminate as the jail sentences imposed by the regime.

In the protean oral medium the underground Group of Ten who challenge obscurantist power pin their faith to the few signs that exist since there is nothing else with which to fix the flux, or even prove the existence, of human experience. Signs are crucial for the objective notation of reality: they mark limits, define and identify; they certify reality by keeping an evidential record of people and events which insists that things happened. Thus it is no surprise that all those who oppose the dictatorship in the book are members of the younger generation of university-educated literati and that there is, subsequently, a diametric opposition of a progressive sophisticated literacy to a primitive reactionary orality. We hear nothing from the Group of Ten about the outspoken oral poets who also fell victim to the Barre regime[9] and it is not until the Dulman episode of *Sardines* that Farah demonstrates an awareness of the oral mode's revolutionary possibilities. All of the rebels in *Sweet and Sour Milk* are revolutionaries of the written word, which they see as posing the greatest threat to an oralized power system. Thus Loyaan entertains the naive hope that a written public statement will refute the lies fabricated about his brother by his father; Ibrahim trusts optimistically that "the written word, more powerful than the gun, will frighten them"; and Soyaan, who kept his official memos short because of the semi-illiteracy of the ruling oligarchy, seems from the scraps of his writings that survive to have shared this perhaps deluded faith in the subversive potential of the written word, not realizing that the real sources of power lay elsewhere. The fate in store for literate protest against unalphabeted tyranny is, in fact, sounded proleptically during the retrospective beach scene between Soyaan and Margaritta at the beginning of the book, where the narrative voice hints chillingly at a distant police presence just as Soyaan's name is washed from the sand by the tide:

> The solidity of his body in the water's transparency flowed into ripples of fantasy. [...] She wrote his name on the sand. The sea washed away her writing. They silently watched the water recede. He wished he could read her message in the water receding. (pp. 12-13)

Here, in the novel's Prologue - in the dissolving of solid, stable realities into fantasy, the washing away of words, the symbolic erasure of the written text - the pattern for the book is set. What are the implications for written texts - for Farah's own text - in a mode of reality built on oral discourse, where the established codes range from the badly to the barely scripted, the ill-written (in the sense of inauthentic) to the unwritten? What happens to language when nothing is happening - in the sense of being written - in it?

One possible option is for the text to retreat deeper into its "writtenness" and for its peculiarly literary texture to grow denser. *Sweet and Sour Milk*, as one critic has observed, probes its own language, which both *tells* and *is* the story.[10] Partly in imitation of, partly in resistance to the Somali political reality under the dictator, it becomes a darkly hermetic, opaque hieroglyph layered with mysteries, its meanings driven underground into cryptic codes: the John Wain poem scribbled by Soyaan on the back of Marco's photograph; enigmatic signs scratched in the sand by his mistress at his funeral; the mysterious monosyllables dropped down the telephone by Xassan, minimally echoic to thwart the General's Dionysian cave of listening devices; and Soyaan's secret "alphabet of mysteries" (and "mystery of alphabets") - "I/M" (Ibrahim/Medina/ Mulki?) and "M to the power of 2" (Margaritta and Marco, Mogadiscio and Moscow?). Given the paranoid context of persecuted print where written texts are both threatening and threatened, Farah's own narrative develops into a correspondingly obscure and evasive text in the face of the reader's interrogation of it for possible clues, so that the uncertainty of the questing protagonist becomes the reader's own. Much of the text is taken up by questions but they are, in Loyaan's phrase, "Whys and no wherefores [...], endless questions, unprovidable answers." The book itself retreats into Soyaan's secret codes, recreating the atmosphere of confusion and mistrust spread by the General, and, as Ian Adam has observed, the awaited clarifying closure of the political thriller and detective novel encouraged by the book's form is finally dissolved in a polygraphy of possible meanings.[11]

Alternatively, the public oral code begins to infiltrate the written text, which in turn takes on certain selected characteristics of the oral modes of discourse privileged by the regime: notably, the oral narrative's reconstructive and reinventive capacities, its talent for the improvisation of alternative versions in the retelling of tales; its subsequently unstable order of meaning and susceptibility to variation, omission, changes of emphasis and shifts of shape; its vagaries of characterisation and fluid indeterminacy of form; and, most dangerous in the present political context, the interpretative openness that follows inevitably from a form of discourse which is audience-orientated rather than performer-centred. "Must everything be reinterpreted according to the code of clan, class or group-interest? [...] Let everybody interpret things as they wished," laments Loyaan, despairing at the systematic misinterpretation of the facts of his brother's life by their policeman-father and the police-state that he serves (p. 138-39). In this novel lives, like plots coming and going in an epic narrative, are reimaginable and, in theory, infinitely interpretable.

A glance at patterns of oral performance and response might be instructive at this point. Jacqueline Bardolph, comparing the allusive epigraphic vignettes that open the chapters of *Sweet and Sour Milk* with the stage directions of Farah's play *Yussuf and his Brothers*, notes that this quite normal African mode of discourse, though it relies on sign and code, "also demands active participation from the audience in the establishment of meaning" insofar as some significances "remain open or only come to life in the situation of communication" and that "some incidents are susceptible in their own terms of many layers of interpretation."[12] *Sweet and Sour Milk* is, in fact, full of multi-layered, miniature oral "texts" of this kind, requiring an audience's complementary interpretation: for example, the symbolic vignettes of weather and skyscape which open the chapters, and the recurring epigraphic refrain of rival poisons fed to an infant who is denied his mother's milk. The latter may be variously construed as the "sour" and "sweet" sides of the Somali temperament, represented by Loyaan and Soyaan, Keynaan and his wives, the General and the Group of Ten; the mixed bag of colonial education, which offsets Keynaan's flat conception of the universe with the rounded, global view but also teaches that Africa had no pre-colonial history; or the successive poisons of colonial and the General's regimes.

The butcher's riddlingly eloquent "text" of the tribal goat, tortured for its own enlightenment before being ritually slaughtered, is of the same order of experience:

> I am training her so that she can grasp the meaning of death before I slaughter her. Your father has, with the money he paid for her head, taught her what it means to be separated from where she was born and her tribal masters. She grasped that being dragged here. Now I've cut the tribal ear. A little later, I shall gladly administer death to her. (p. 209)

Salman Rushdie has a similar passage in *The Satanic Verses*, referring to the Angel Gibreel's decree that

> animals be killed slowly, by bleeding, so that by experiencing their deaths to the full they might arrive at an understanding of the meaning of their lives, for

> it is only at the moment of death that living creatures understand that life has been real, and not a sort of dream.[13]

The dream-like malaise of Farah's everyday Somali reality, with its ever-present threat of death, is of some relevance here, but there seems to be more at stake in this than the Koranic meanings. The butcher's parable is perhaps most obviously and immediately interpretable as a pat exemplum for Loyaan who determines not to be surprised by anything: "Unlike Soyaan whom death had surprised, Loyaan would be ready for it" (p. 208). But a few pages on Margaritta corrects "this wrong notion that Soyaan was unprepared for death when it came. [...] He wasn't surprised by death" (p. 225). In the light of this information, Soyaan himself becomes the goat in the fable, either as a sacrificial martyr to a spurious revolution or as a scapegoat, focusing the wrath of the regime on the rising tide of anti-Soviet activities and issuing a warning to the other members of the Group of Ten. Alternatively, the butcher's text represents a broader image of modern Somalia, decaying and moribund under a tribal patriarch, and of its Western-educated sons, uprooted from their birthplaces but still psychologically scarred by their tribal heritage and facing a choice of deaths: the atrophy of exile or torture and execution at the hands of the same tribalism in militarized form. Of course, the episode may be merely a gratuitous exhibition of personal sadism. Beyond each of these readings, and encompassing all of them, it stands reflexively as a sinister paradigm of Somali reality under an obscurantist dictator and of the regime's fundamentally uninterpretable political imbecility, unintelligible in any terms other than those of personal power-mania.

In the next novel the oralist Idil, the matriarchal representative of the General on the domestic front, is seen to "thread-draw in her mind a past with patterns different from the one she had the intention of re-narrating. [...] Idil counted the number of holes she had to jump in order to form a pattern."[14] In the tangled webs of both the General's and Idil's oral texts, the "holes" or lacunae, the interpretive spaces and absences around the words, are as important as the words themselves in the forming of patterns. The oral mode is, in a very post-modernist way, an uncentred or off-centred mode of discourse, subject to the law of the excluded middle,[15] and there is in *Sweet and Sour Milk* a prevailing motif of uncentredness which ties together its political themes, its protagonist's psychological and philosophical dilemmas, and its indexings to oral conventions. The ontological crisis is not merely a personal phenomenon but is part of a broader national and continental malaise.

In Margaritta's polemical monologue and in Loyaan's reflected responses Somalia (and modern Africa which it serves as a microcosm of) is itself envisaged as a centreless and featurless void into which anything can be put and of which anything can be made.[16] It is a space inhabited by so many inauthentic foreign and indigenous presences but without any inner core of identity. After the British and Italian colonizers come "KGBs and CIA espionage networks" to take up residence alongside "wizardry and witchcraft and hair-burning rites of sorcery" and the "make-believe" lives of Western-educated elites who turn Africa into "a textbook reproduction of European values and western thinking" (pp. 124, 148). The history of the ancient European world as presented through the twins' Italian education is a mass of solid documentation: "history as chiselled out of the harshness of rocks, come the Greeks themselves, the Sicilians, the Normans, the Arabs" (p. 168). But at school "they were told *they* had no history" (p. 131). Its past envisaged as an oral blank, Somalia has no history or, alternatively, its history exists in too many variant versions for any of it to be certain. The nation's preliterate, precolonial history is conceived as an endlessly reinvented narrative, improvised over a factual vacuum and on which each successive regime plays its own variations before an obliging mass-audience. Its more recent, postcolonial history is reconstituted at the whim of patriarchal dictators, frequently in terms of the flat, cartoon-like fictions that inform Keynaan's traditional pre-heliocentric view of the universe - "the flat universe of Father's calculable dimensions" as against "the oval-shaped one of solar and lunar evolutions and revolutions" (p. 106). But even these are imitative of foreign propagandist practices: Loyaan refers us to the Hungarian Uprising and Prague Spring, and to the "official" government version's polarization of the population into heinous reactionary rebels and heroic "revolutionary" armies (pp. 103, 106). Soyaan, Loyaan observes wryly, died "of revolutionary heroism."

Somalia's political uncentredness is matched by the decentred, satellite-lives of its intellectuals. Margaritta, limiting the relevance of her past affair with the Minister in the matter of Soyaan's death, marginalizes her influence - "I am not central to all that has taken place" (p. 228) - while Beydan has a recurring dream in which she is not only not the centre-point but is not even there, in which no dreamer is present to direct and focus the dream. The real Soyaan is absent from the funeral celebrations that remake him into a myth: "Soyaan [was] the centre of this festivity although, just like Beydan in her dream, he too wasn't there" (p. 231). Because there is no route by which his writings might pass into speech in the regime's repressive, text-exclusive oral culture, Soyaan's fate will be to be remembered not by their complex truths but by the oral slogans that refashion him into a revolutionary hero (commenting ironically in his Memorandum on the banal oralization of history, Soyaan notes that Mussolini is remembered not by the deeds recorded in the history books but by the trite quip about making trains run on time that has passed into the folk-memory). The indeterminacy of oral history makes it difficult to distinguish between the true and the legendary, the real and the imaginary. In what sense, for example, can Soyaan be said to have existed except as a mythical property of the government, a revolutionary artifact like the parks, streets and towering buildings named after him? Loyaan is repeatedly mistaken for his twin and hears Soyaan's voice speaking posthumously inside his head, tempering his impetuosity with its secrecy and discretion, until he begins to wonder, like his mother Qumman, if he and his dead twin are not really the same person, a single composite character or Siamese soul: "One in two: Loyaan and Soyaan," says Ladan of her two brothers. The new national fathers, in effect, refuse to authorize their sons' existences by denying them a stable political reality and offering in its place only a multiplicity of versions.

The manufacturer of this many-versioned malaise and the ringmaster of its peculiar epistemological circus is, of course, the General. In theory, Somalia's Islamic militarism is centred on key signs in a written code: its politics on the Revolutionary Council's constitution and its religion on the Koran. In practice, however, the nation's political father has substituted for the constitution his own personality - "Have I ever introduced myself to you, young man? I *am* the constitution," the General roars at Soyaan - and he has bowdlerized the Koran into a collection of slogans and hackneyed praise-songs ("There is no General but our General") parrotted by his military stooges, a debasement that leaves the original text corrupted beyond restitution (for Loyaan at Soyaan's funeral, the Koran stands "open and unreadable"). The effect, Soyaan notes, has been to decentre Somalia's political reality by placing phrases like "radical governments" and "revolutionary socialism" in the "punctuational accessories" of parentheses and inverted commas that hold them at a remove from the real thing.

A similar indeterminacy informs characterization. Under the stage-management of the General, "Mulki", the sister of Ibrahim who allegedly types Soyaan's secret memorandum, is an entire character enclosed in inverted commas. She is wholly "oral" in conception, a character for whom there is neither documentary evidence, in photographic or written records, within the contexts of realism nor any other form of narrative confirmation. We are given only others' representations and reported versions of Mulki's doings and never meet the woman herself. She suffers - indeed, she exists - on hearsay alone, and on mainly doubtful hearsay at that: of Keynaan and Ahmed-Wellie, government informers and spies; and of a tribally antagonistic receptionist at the government office where Loyaan goes in futile pursuit of Soyaan's death certificate (possibly a spy recruited from the tribal group most hostile to the General to divert suspicion). It is Loyaan who in fact supplies the unnamed typist first mentioned by Keynaan with the name "Mulki," though he has previously never heard either of Ibrahim or his sister, and it is never completely clear that "Mulki Musse" and Ibrahim's sister are one and the same person. There seems to be a lacunae in the text that leaves unclear the source of the name, which Loyaan then hunts down in ministerial files that disclaim all knowledge of its owner's existence. Is the character an invention of Keynaan's and Ahmed-Wellie's to mislead Loyaan? Later the dubious doctor is called out to tend a blindfolded female torture-victim and to deal with "a mad case of euthanasia administered to a woman." Are either of these Mulki? Ahmed-Wellie says not, but Loyaan disbelieves his claim to know the woman. In the "badly written farce" staged for Loyaan by the Minister to the Presidency in the interrogation scene "Mulki" is represented by an incompetent actress, wheeled onto the set at ministerial cue to protest that she has been neither arrested nor maltreated and promising to be there at the airport to wave him off to the foreign diplomatic post which the embarrassed regime has hastily created for him. If there is such a person as Mulki, it is unlikely that this is she, but depending upon oral testimony alone, we have no way of knowing whether there really is such a person and, if there is, whether she has indeed been arrested and has broken under torture. Both Mulki's torture and Soyaan's fatal injection are, moreover, presented in the form of frenzied dream and delirium in the protagonal consciousness - Soyaan raves of "pale, ghostly beings which jabbed [him] with needles" (p. 17) - so that unreality is deliberately conferred upon them, blurring the true and the imagined. Thus we can no more distinguish the real from the merely represented Mulki than we can the real Soyaan from the mythical revolutionary artifact. Both are "unwritten" entities, not figures in Farah's written text but figments of the General's oral scenario.

In the novel the General is repeatedly imaged as a cunningly false artificer, the constructor of "showy pieces of tumorous architecture" and "monuments of false hope." Farah has characterised him somewhat differently, however, in his essay "Why I Write," where he claims that "Somalia was a badly written play" and "Siyad Barre was its author. [...] he was also the play's main actor, its centre and theme; as an actor-producer, he played all the available roles."[17] In *Sweet and Sour Milk* he appears to have conceived Somali political reality as a grotesque parody of orature and the more precise analogy that suggests itself in the narrative is of the General as a species of debased oral performer. He is presented as a malevolent, diabolically inventive kind of oral historian, ringing endless surprises and variations on the theme of silencing dissidents, fabricating imagined alternatives for the lives of his trampled victims and, with the help of men like Keynaan, breathing life into lies that travesty their real ones. An astute and wily performer, he serves up for his nation's oral epics, sung by his "griots in green", new "heroes and legendary figures about whom one tells stories to children and future generations" (p. 183). In Farah's dark parody, however, there is none of the usual reciprocity between teller and listener. Instead of the griot's self-effacing assumption of a common identity with his audience and his instilling of a common sense of reality into it, the aim is, through sheer imposition of the dictatorial will, to render the audience's hold on these things unsure. The listener, Loyaan learns, must make himself alertly receptive to new variations and impervious to surprise; he must "plot, plan, wriggle and struggle the best he could, and let nothing surprise him" (p. 208). But the General's ideal audience consists not of active, contributing participants but of passive assenters who can rearrange themselves into any shape required or, alternatively, have none to begin with: brainwashed buffoons mouthing official dogma; political stooges like Keynaan, men with no core of identity who will stoop to any baseness to ingratiate themselves with power; and beggars, who are so compliantly impressionable and manipulable that it is impossible to surprise them. "Here was an audience willing to hear anything," says Loyaan of the latter. Appropriately, those who are most attuned to the General's protean oral reality are themselves adept shape-changers who, in one symbolic scene, actually transform themselves before Loyaan's eyes in response to the visitations of power:

> The beggars no longer resembled the remnants of a plane-crash. No, they were the passengers of a third-class train, stirring forward, jerking, shaking, speaking. [...] Power had chosen to visit them. The Minister to the Presidency and his entourage of cars and security men had arrived. (p. 229)

Loyaan notes that beggars, unlike Beydan, Soyaan and Margaritta, "are the centre of their dreams," but it is a hollow centre, a void where identity should be, a blank ready to be moulded into any form. In the centreless world of oral-based totalitarian power, the beggar becomes the image for the average citizen.

Sweet and Sour Milk, Ian Adam argues at the end of his penetrating article "The Murder of Soyaan Keynaan," uses the quasi-paternalist forms of the detective novel, and the mystery-suspense and political thriller, only to depart from them, and it does so, I think, because its ontology is essentially more complex and sophisticated than theirs. Adam expresses a reluctance to reduce the novel's rejection of final answers to the hermeneutic scepticism of the *nouveau roman* and thus to "postmodernize" Farah's text in any hardline way, arguing that the novel's comparative lack of closure is more ethical than epistemological in origin. Farah, he contends, "clearly sets the notion of collective activity, of collaboration and consensus" against the detective novel's relatively egocentric and authoritarian notion of a single leader and rescuer (a father-figure) who "ties up all the loose ends."[18] It is certainly true that, even though the clandestine organization has been decimated at the end of this novel and lies dormant in the next one, the ideal of collective resistance to one-man-rule is kept alive as a positive force throughout the trilogy. It is also true, of course, that the figure of authority, the father-figure in Farah's novel, could hardly fill the detective's role of "tier up of loose ends" since he himself is the creator of them. Here the patriarchal messiah-figure is himself the mystifier-criminal element in the plot, the fabricator of an obscurantist order of reality, and there exists no other authoritative hermeneutic agent to counter his fabrications and provide a definitive, authorized version of events. Thus it is to be wondered (and Adam partly concedes so much) if Farah really intends us to be much closer at the end of the book than at the beginning to a true account of the events surrounding Soyaan's death. Is Farah not undermining the whole idea that a knowable and verifiable personal reality is still discernible behind a coercive system of mystificatory political representations?

Even if the novel's vaporous, polymorphous political reality is not in excess of the requirements of the detective and political thriller genres, the highly poetic meteorological matter in which it is reflected surely is. Here the hypnotic, hallucinatory aspects of Farah's style - which occasionally result in some inept writing[19] - are much in evidence. Cloud formations, the night's phantasmagoric skyscapes, and the sun, which "poured its blazing vapouriness upon everything", constantly assume different shapes - camels, trees, garments, pillars, skulls - to the imagination playing its variations upon them. Like the regime's political enormities, they keep the beholder guessing, keeping always one step ahead of Loyaan's imagination which walks "the untrod landscape of the unknowable" (p. 59). But when night falls "in a veil of darkness," Loyaan discovers, at one of the novel's crucial reflexive moments, that the art-work is really shoddy, the scenery badly painted, and that, like the political order of which it is a metaphor, there is really nothing behind it: "Empty at my touch like a soap-bubble, everything reducible to nought, nothing. Inexistent at my remembering, like a dream" (p. 143). Somali reality under the dictator constitutes not so much a slippery and confusing multiplicity of signs as a signless void, providing no forms in which coherent meanings can be expressed:

> The night unrolled like a cotton thread, unfolding inch by inch; the night wove words of thready thoughts; the night stitched for him a blanket of comfort and warmth. [...] Every movement he heard had a meaning, and if it didn't he gave it one. The security men were following him and making sure he stayed indoors, in one version. [...] Then, right before Loyaan's and the world's eyes, all suddenly began to disintegrate like a worn-out piece of cloth a thick set of fingers has pulled asunder. (pp. 205-06, 210-11).

The sun's sudden dismantling of the "fabric of schemata", the text written upon the night by Loyaan's imagination, is indirectly an image of Farah's own text deconstructively unstitching itself and running out unresolvedly amid a welter of conflicting oral testimony (the motif is repeated in the epigraph to Chapter 5, in which a child's toy falls apart at the removal and misplacement of a nail). What looks like an unfolding of meaning turns out to be an unravelling of the entire fabric in which meaning should reside: the novel's ontological barriers are themselves breached and the proliferation of "versions" in the place of verities precludes the literary representation of reality as a series of discoverable indivisible truths. Perhaps it is not surprising that Loyaan, as a character within the narrative's realistic frame, comes increasingly to rely upon physical instinct and touch for his sense of reality. The starkness of Soyaan's corpse, Margaritta's erotic presence, his almost visceral hatred of his father and his intuitive distrust of Ahmed-Wellie become the guiding touchstones for his existence.

All of this naturally problematizes the epistemological status of Farah's own text. "You always lose hold of your own reality," the dying Soyaan was informed by his mother, and those who try to track down the facts of the dead man's life - Loyaan, the reader - find their own hold upon the world weakened. As Loyaan is unable to unravel the butcher's tortuous text of the goat, so the novel's narrative plot is unable to unravel the details and motives of the political-criminal plot to murder and mythologize Soyaan, and it subsequently develops, mimetically, into a correspondingly evasive text for the reader. The narrative's defensiveness before the reader's cross-examination of it for clues imitates and re-enacts Loyaan's suspicions of "friends" whom, for one reason or another, he is afraid to tell everything he knows (including even his sister Ladan, for whom knowledge may mean danger). The result is that the feverish confusion and insecurity fostered by the regime are recreated by the narrative's own refusal to clarify and its subsequent withdrawal into cryptic codes like the ones employed by Soyaan. In a more insidious way, the narrative consciousness behaves as if it were itself being plotted against and interrogated by an implied reader, looking over the writer's shoulder like some hermeneutic thought-police - hence the text's plethora of echoing, unanswered questions and inquisitorial exhortations ("Address yourself to the question!"). D. R. Ewen comments astutely that "one feels relieved to have got out of the book safely."[20]

The oral-based conspiracy against Soyaan is, in the last analysis, unwritten and therefore unwritable. We are told in the final chapter that only Ladan, who has hidden Soyaan's writings in a place known to herself alone, will be able to resume control of Loyaan's narrative quest and restitch the true text of Soyaan's life: "Ladan is that Solomonic thread which connects all, which stitches the holes its needle has made. Follow the hints of that thread, follow it with patience" (p. 225). It is Ladan who, significantly, is left at the end of the book holding the child born out of Beydan's death and who names him Soyaan, thus implying that Keynaan has been given a replacement for his dead son and causing him to falter momentarily in his prayers. Ladan seems therefore to hold the key to Soyaan's posthumous future. Yet she is, puzzlingly, one of the few characters who fails to reappear or receive any substantial mention in the next two volumes of the trilogy.[21] Subsequently, the precise whereabouts of Soyaan's scripts (and written texts like this one) are left uncertain. "The sky is too high to reach and hide them in," Loyaan tells his sister, "the earth too earthy and too exposed and the boxes are not sufficiently secretive" (p. 224).

There are, however, some positive poles of resistance in the book to the frightening indeterminacy of the Somali political reality. One of these is the lush poetic lyricism which, though itself part of the phantasmagoria, also endows weather and light, sunrise and the descent of night, with a physical and earthily sensual dimension. The recurring images of wombs, fertilizing sperm, foetuses and eggs are not merely symbolic of the aborted hopes of the 1969 Revolution or of the faith in the future which is pinned to the creative energies of Somalia's women. They also appear to represent the private bodily and sexual realities over which the state has no claim of ownership, that tender pragmatism of the flesh which becomes the only touchstone, the only tangible thing individuals have to hold onto in the enveloping malaise. The other point of resistance to oral chaos is an aesthetic one: namely, Farah's own defiantly ordered textual patterns which impose clear definition and design even upon a mad and meaningless world. Striking among these, in the light of the close physical intimacy of Somali family life, are the analogic devices and parallelisms through which Farah, in surreal dream-sequences, couples brothers and sisters, pairs off parents and children, and marks whole family groups and modes of parenthood (a feature that will become more pronounced in *Sardines*). Underlying patterns also emerge from the epigraphic subtexts: images of a stray weed caught in a whirlwind, an ant in a flood, a butterfly destroyed by a child, a bedridden centenarian and a baby abandoned in a garbage bin repeat the refrain of the powerlessness and helplessness of isolated individuals before overwhelming forces (the members of the Group of Ten are dangerously isolated, each one knowing the identity of only one other member). Perhaps most striking, however, are the grand microcosmic metaphors which draw together in a single swoop a number of the book's key thematic threads. Thus the recurring childhood memory of Keynaan tyrannically bursting the atlas-covered, egg-like ball played with by the twins gathers many motifs at once. It encompasses the rival cosmologies of fathers and sons and their respective codes of unthinking despotism and free inquiry, narrow bigotry and global vision. On the one hand there is the full "roundness" of human complexity, gained from knowledge and experience; on the other, the "flatness" of propagandist lies and the cartoon-caricature that Keynaan has let himself become. The creative potency of the fertile brain is opposed to the anti-creative brute force of the "Grand Patriarch," for whom the "round" world is "an egg that awaits your breaking it" and who chooses to "breathe life" not into his dead son but into a lie that traduces him. Linked with this key metaphor is another of the novel's positives, Farah's faith in education and his implied belief that truth will out. In defiance of their father's contempt for women and his "flat" mental cosmology, the twins educate their sister Ladan, telling her stories from all parts of the globe - India, China, Iceland, Arabia - and feeding "her small brain on figures round, complete and open-ended" (p. 110) to enlarge her knowledge and view of the world.

These powerful images are the things that stay in the mind as the narrative dissolves at the end of *Sweet and Sour Milk* and Beydan, as in her dream, dies delivering a child called Soyaan, who may or may not unearth the facts about his dead namesake:

> Twenty years later, for all one knew, a Soyaan who survived Beydan's death in childbirth might walk a street named after a brother Soyaan knighted by a false revolution, made a hero in order to hide in the virtuosity of the generosity of politics. (p. 218)[22]

Exactly what is delivered, achieved or brought to fruition at the end of the book and what value it has are left unclear. It may be the new offspring's gesture of hope for the future; the recovered truth about Soyaan or the promised revival of the written word that will give it expression; Margaritta's thesis on "The Burgeoning of the National Security Service as an Institution of Power in Africa"; or this book, which contains that thesis and which, as the written record of courage and integrity, poses the greatest threat to the mystifications of oral-based totalitarian power in Somalia.

CHAPTER FIVE
Mothers and Daughters: *Sardines*

Farah has said in an interview that *Sweet and Sour Milk* is about those who do not compromise whilst *Sardines*, the next novel in the trilogy, is about those who do.[1] Switching focus from fathers and sons to mothers and daughters, and from patriarchs to matriarchs, *Sardines* plots the paths of that compromise. The crucial compromising agent, however, remains the power of the familial and domestic context, now claustrophobically intensified by the helplessness of the Somali woman's position in society. Women such as Medina and Ebla own houses in Somalia but are allowed no public or political presence; drawing their strength from quite different sources, these two are in fact untypically independent figures in a culture where the position of women is negotiated entirely by their fathers, husbands and brothers. In such a society it is permissable for a rape victim to be regarded by her assailants, as is the woman Amina, as a mere appendage of her father, and for the crime to remain unpunishable and politically non-existent because of the low evaluation of the victim.

Following the elimination of Soyaan and Loyaan by death and exile, it is now the turn of the women in Farah's overlapping, discontinuous narrative to take up the struggle against the regime, but in *Sardines* active resistance has given way to a beleagured impotence and frustration, and the protests are more gestural than effectual: editing the General's speeches in the national newspaper and abandoning house and husband (Medina), withdrawal from the national swimming team (Sagal), and, more dangerously, painting the dawn with anti-government slogans (Cadar and Hindiya). Accordingly, the punishments and penances meted out to a group styled as "inferior beings" by the regime are more moderate than death, prison or exile. These constitute, for the central figure Medina, virtual house arrest; for the now middle-aged Ebla, the silence of the self-censoring private conscience, "worn on the inside"; and for Xaddia, Medina's sister-in-law, the pseudo-exile of work as an air hostess.

The plot of *Sardines*, after Loyaan's labyrinthine quest in the previous book, is relatively simple, though a summary of the plot alone does scant justice to the novel's poetic intricacy or to the complexity of its intellectual debate. Removed from her position of editor and placed under a banning order for tampering with the regime's national editorials, Medina flees with her eight-year-old daughter Ubax to the house of her brother Nasser, leaving her house and husband at the mercy of her tyrannical mother-in-law Idil. The latter has threatened to have Ubax circumcised and her husband Samater, to avert a political purge of his kinsmen, has reluctantly accepted a position in the government and has thus compromised Medina, who is writing a book criticizing the regime. Idil promptly brings into the house a distant cousin as a replacement wife for her son, whereupon Samater throws her out and, in the process, brings the wrath of the regime down upon his head: he is stripped of his office, arrested and brutally interrogated. Medina, meanwhile, imparts doctrine to and debates tactics with her intellectual proteges and, like one such disciple (Ebla's daughter Sagal), continues to influence events from the sidelines whilst others become the casualties of the struggle against tyranny. Not she but her brother Nasser and the singer Dulman are arrested and sentenced to death for disseminating subversive material; in parallel fashion, her pupil Sagal stands agonizing by whilst her competitors in the Somali swimming team are arrested for painting incendiary slogans. In the novel's uncertain ending, Samater is released from captivity and returns to reconstitute the broken nuclear family, putting at least one house back in order: "Medina, Samater, and Ubax behaved as though they needed one another's company [...]"[2]

Sardines teases out and pinpoints unerringly all the subterfuges and hypocrisies of compromise. Accepting the post of Minister of Constructions to prevent the decimation of his tribesmen, Samater tries to hide behind the pretence that he is really helping to moderate tyranny from within but knows in his heart that truth must be owned:

> We the intellectuals are the betrayers; we the so-called intellectuals are the entrance the foreign powers use so as to dominate, designate, name and label; we the intellectuals are the ones who tell our people lies. [...] We are the ones that keep dictators in power. (p. 72)

The indecisive Sagal finds her thunder stolen by her rivals and, already pregnant by a visiting West Indian photographer who has compromised with the regime, can do no more than feebly withdraw from the championship, whereupon another girl is immediately nominated in her place. Meanwhile, Medina, by using the national newspaper as a vehicle of protest within three days of taking up the editorship, does exactly what is expected of her and acts out the General's scenario for her silencing: "Medina was offered the pen with which she wrote herself off," comments the astute Ebla (p. 41). By then abandoning Samater to the monomaniacal Idil, she succeeds only in precipitating the conflict between husband and mother-in-law which will lead to Samater's public disgrace and detention. That these things happen as a result of her own actions and lie upon her own conscience seem not to occur to her for the greater part of the book, through which Medina steers a charmed and blithely unconcerned passage. Protected as she is by her privileged position as one of the country's leading writers and intellectuals and aware that the worst that can happen to her are banning orders and sexual harrassment from Samater's kinsmen, she can afford to lambast the General as "backward and fascist" and "an uneducated imbecile" and do much else that is politically simplistic and productive of nothing except her own self-glorification. At the extremes of the picture, moving beyond compromise to total sell-out, are the Italian journalist Sandra and the black American Atta, respectively the credulous white stooge and black spy of the "revolution" and both mistresses of the same government minister. These two connive at tribal elitism, clan nepotism and the Islamic subjugation of women in the name of Marxism and Africanity ("my race remembers"), both of which the dictatorship lays claim to at different times.

Medina's consciousness, exasperatingly, occupies the largest space in this portrait of embattled Somali womanhood (characters such as Sandra and Atta, who appear in only a couple of scenes, have virtually no existence outside of her characterisation of them and seem to exist merely to prove true what she says about them). Medina's status in the novel is subsequently problematic, the authorial perspective on her discordantly open-ended, and even the image-motifs associated with her full of rival possibilities: the Muslim religious meaning of her name is "city of righteousness" while in its contracted form, Mina, it signifies "the place where pillars are stoned, a symbol of Satan" (p. 146).[3]

Much can be and has been said in defence of Medina. As Patricia Alden observes of her responses to Xaddia, Medina's first priority is the battle for the survival of women against tyrannical domestic and political regimes like Idil's and the General's, which causes her to put the feminist cause before family loyalties.[4] On a similarly positive note, Rosemary Colmer argues that Medina uses her manipulative powers in a constructive way: namely, to engineer a situation in which Samater is forced to take cognizance of and confront his mother's intolerable meddling, from which she has hitherto screened and cushioned him.[5] On the other hand, Farah warns us in the early pages of Medina's egotistical possessiveness towards her daughter and the self-absorbed ideological purity of all her actions. She appears, initially, to leave husband and home not because of her desire to reacquaint Samater with the reality of Idil's tyranny (this is one of a number of retrospective motives) or even because of the latter's threat to circumcize Ubax, but because she cannot write a book critical of the government whilst married to and living in the same house as one of its ministers. Very little account, it seems, is taken by her of the extenuating factors of Samater's dilemma (Farah does not give space to any introspections on these), and this raises the awkward question of whether she expected him to allow his clansmen to be wiped out. In terms of hard facts, moreover, Medina's challenges to the regime are hardly effective actions; rather, they are flamboyant and self-indulgent ideological gestures which leave the enemy (Idil, the General) in possession of the spoils (Samater, Somalia) and which, as Xaddia observes, others usually pay the price of:

> "You pawn and pawn and pawn until there is nothing or nobody left to put up to auction. Yesterday, it was Samater; today, Nasser and Dulman; tomorrow - who knows? - maybe it's my turn; the day after tomorrow, Sagal. When will you stop being obstinate and start seeing reason? Will you never concede or accept defeat?" (p. 246)

This needs some qualification. As Alden points out,[6] Xaddia's anguish is the biased response of a family member and injured party, and her emotions carry her beyond the verifiable facts: Medina is not directly to blame for the arrests of Dulman and Nasser, who are engaged in independent actions and are seized in a general crackdown, though her defiant, attention-attracting posturings do tend to exacerbate the climate of hostility towards other known dissidents. The problem remains, nonetheless, that so much of the narrative is presented from the perspective of Medina's intransigent idealism and coloured by her priggish self-righteousness that these, particularly in the closing paragraphs of the book, come to have a ring of doctrinal finality and authorial approval:

> Medina a hostess? Why, when she altered the position of the chair the house fell in on her and the ground below her shook with seismic determination. No, she wasn't a guest any more. She was a full and active participant in the history of her country. (p. 250)

Such passages have prompted some critics, notably Barbara Turfan,[7] to ask why Farah is so slow to censure his characters' shortcomings and inadequacies and to wonder if he is sufficiently aware of them. Has Medina, from the confined seclusion of her private room, really shaken the Somali earth on which her house stands? What has she finally achieved apart from the private fulfilment of a renuclearized family and how long will it be before the General takes punitive action against his disgraced minister? Is Farah's closing chorus of praise genuine or ironic?

If the answer is not a simple one it is because the sealed sardine tin of Somali society, denying women a public outlet, forces them inward into a suffocating intimacy and this generates such a tangled network of inter-relationships and conflicts - personal, political and religious - that no single character or set of relations can be considered and evaluated in isolation. *Sardines* is Farah's most formidably planned, patterned and argumentative novel (though what is finally proved may not be clear). It pairs off mothers and daughters (Medina and Fatima, Sagal and Ebla, Ubax and Medina) more painstakingly than the brothers and sisters of the previous book and breaks down a large cast of characters into couples facing each other over poles of interest which define their identities and oppositions: Medina and Idil over Ubax; Idil and Samater over Medina; Medina and the General, like lizards in their "varanian dance of death", over the destiny of Somalia. In his analogical treatment of character, and most especially of Medina, lies the full complexity of Farah's vision, for the oppositions drawn up are complementary rather than diametric or absolute and reveal continuity at the heart of apparent contrast. Packed inescapably together as they are in their claustrophobic casing, all the women are aspects of one another, forcibly alike to the extent that they are all in the same tin: the outcome is that all become, in some way, part of a single repressed but irrepressible female personality. In this novel the reader is given not a collection of individuals but a composite portrait of Somali womanhood in which character is interdependent and interpenetrative.

Farah has said that "everyone contains different things - the woman in the child, the man in the woman and so on", that in his novels "an intellectual and psychological debate is going on between two selves - the woman's self in the man, the man's self in the woman."[8] Thus Westernization brings out the latent feminine in Samater and the masculine in Medina, a theme to be explored further in the interchanging sexual roles of Salaado and Hilaal, Misra and Askar in *Maps*. The motherless intellectual figurehead Medina sees herself as complementing the fatherless athletic torchbearer Sagal, as the childless parent and parentless child will do in *Maps*. Sagal is also seen as teenage protege and proxy by Medina (with Ubax as a younger version) and, under her mentorship, as successor and inheritor in the struggle against dictatorship. Even in the novel's sliding scale of maternal authority, which ranges from Idil's psychopathic domination through the moderate Fatima's non-interference to Ebla's enlightened tolerance, the categories prove to be more fluid than fixed. Hence the liberal adaptability which we might expect from the free Somali nomad we find instead in the purdah-strangled Yemeni woman from the Arabic tradition (Fatima), and the obsessive rigidity looked for in the purdah-victim is discovered to be entrenched in the nomad (Idil).

Similarly, Sagal and Medina partake of the natures of their opponents. Sagal invokes the "sacrificial element of history - martyrdom" in her celebration of her rival swimmers' heroics, thus espousing the regime's own "mother-martyr mentality" which she affects to despise and incurring her mother's pragmatic rebuke: "I would say they succeeded if they wrote their message and got away" (p. 128). Medina, in Samater's reverie, is identified with a cosmopolitan eclecticism which clutches at the flowers of different cultures but prefers not to be rooted in any of them, and there is some justification in Gerald Moore's argument that such a person, not deeply in and of the society but wilfully seeking "a life defined like the boundaries of a property", has little claim to its intellectual leadership.[9] Yet the truth is that, for all her foreign education, Medina's attitudes and temperament are rooted deeper in Somali culture than she herself is aware of. She is described in the beginning as "unbending", as the female equivalent of her father Barkhadle: "She was as confident as a patriarch in the rightness of all her decisions" (p. 5). Although Farah would appear to have a preference for the nuclear over the extended family and pins his faith to the displacement of authoritarian methods of socialization by egalitarian ones, he demonstrates that the single-parent variant of the nuclear unit can be as dictatorial as the clan-based polygamous one. The freedom which Medina forces prematurely upon Ubax is at times almost as oppressive as the obedience Idil has forced upon Samater, her emotional and intellectual tyranny over her daughter as stifling as its physical counterpart, and it is perhaps no accident that Farah's metaphor for the freshly-translated world classics force-fed to her daughter - "she gave them to her hot like maize cakes from the oven" (p. 3) - is taken straight from Idil's own entrepreneurial undertakings, supporting herself "by baking maize cakes on commission from a restaurant" (p. 7). In a country of pontifical parents, Medina terrorizes her young daughter with knowledge, as does Idil with the circumcisional knife, and uses English and Italian to place her in a linguistic purdah which is the cultural equivalent of Fatima's religious one. Her Idil-like employment of manipulative powers to interfere with and rearrange the lives of others (Samater, Sagal and, to a lesser extent, Nasser and Dulman) casts her, in fact, as a new kind of matriarch.

"You are a prisoner of your principles, Medina," her mother observes shrewdly. "I am a prisoner of tradition, that I won't deny. One is always the prisoner of one thing or another" (p. 144). Compulsively ideologizing everything, Medina - and Sagal under her tutelage - fall victims to a confusion of the personal and the political that has become a standard feature of life in a state where it is not only no longer possible to challenge the dictator's powers but it is not even possible to disentangle personal affairs from his stranglehold on public life. Thus Sagal is tricked by her buoyant imagination into interpreting even her seduction of Wentworth George as a political act and wonders absurdly if she should "have a child to prick the nation's conscience with guilt. [...] I felt it my national duty to keep the man company for that one night, and so I slept with him" (pp. 116, 129). Clearly Sagal has learned well from Medina, in whose doctrinaire vision the whole of reality is political and all evils derive from and are to be explained in terms of the General's personality: "The General is who I blame. For everything" (p. 140).

"Too simplistic, too categoric," the author allows Samater his doubts, though Farah himself is not without his "Medinizing" tendencies. Farah has said that he has "used women as a symbol for Somalia because, when the women are free, then and only then can we talk about a free Somalia",[10] - which renders suspect all feminine genderings of a "free Somalia" (or a free Somali Ogaden in the later *Maps*) for as long as women are enslaved. Elsewhere he has said: "I see women as the symbol of the subjugated self in everyone of us."[11] Medina herself, of course, is a rather weak symbol of the subjugated national self since she is too Western-internationalist in her orientation, too privileged and protected a member of the elite, and too little oppressed as a woman. Nevertheless, the general enslavement of Somali women can be seen as instrumental in, and therefore analogous to, the political repression of the whole Somali people insofar as, at an immediate practical level, the immensely powerful influence of women on the young is capable of damaging the national psyche and adversely affecting the nation's destiny if it is exercised by a class of people who are continually violated and degraded (a theme to be pursued in *Maps*). It is at a more abstract and doctrinaire level, however, that the Medina-Sagal theorem translates women victimized by clan patriarchy into metaphors for

Somalia under the heel of tribal dictatorship. For them, and perhaps for Farah too, the issue at stake here is not economic class oppression (from his treatment of Sandra, he would appear to have few Marxist sympathies), but the oppression of women by patriarchal tribal oligarchies and of Somalia by the regime, which two things are at times so closely allied as to be virtually indistinguishable. The masses, women and children, "like any inferior beings [...] must be kept guessing," said Medina's grandfather, anticipating the General (p. 140). What the clan does to women the clannish dictator does to the nation, and the implied corollary is that freedom from one will therefore spell freedom from the other, though this does not necessarily follow: Somalia is at last rid of the General but whether this will have much effect on the position of women is yet to be seen.

Hence, we find in *Sardines* a swift movement from microcosm to macrocosm in the two powerful anecdotes of Amina's unpunished rape and the brutal circumcision of the visiting American-Somali girl which together are made to sum up both the plight of Somali womanhood and, more tenuously, the condition of the Somali people, drawn up along broad politico-sexual lines: "The pain is ours, the fat and wealth and power is the men's," comments one of the old women who take Amina in after the assault (p. 119). To her father's comment that this particular rape is political, Amina replies: "But which rape isn't?" The choice of rape as a political weapon against the General by the three young rebels is significant partly because it indicates that they share his sexual politics, but principally in that Farah depicts rape as a re-enactment of the original circumcisional violation of womanhood which is an instrument of tribal patriarchal power over women. Hence the two are associated in the thoughts of Amina, which run the pain of the earlier violation into that of the later - "She had been a virgin, she had been circumcized [...] what pain, what pain!" (p. 119) - and earlier in Medina's comment: "Life for a circumcised woman is a series of de-flowering pains, delivery pains and re-stitching pains" (p. 59). Thus perhaps, in Medina's doctrinaire vision, her two reasons for leaving her home - the protection of Ubax and Samater's forced acceptance of a place in the government - are really the same reason, since societies that terrorize women with circumcision also produce patriarchal monsters like the General. Hence her equation: "Idil *in* the General; the personal *in* the political" (p. 245).

Yet, though the rape *is* a political act and *is* an expression of patriarchal power, it is not wholly or solely this. Throughout his fiction Farah is alert to a pernicious tendency to unmoor metaphors from their vehicles, particularly in the areas of politics and gender, and the rape of Amina is a good example of this dislocative process. The danger of the intellectual extrapolation of abstract "significances" from sensitive subjects such as rape and circumcision, which is a constant feature of the novel's debates, is that the metaphoric correlative of the outrage - moral violation, political coercion - is liable to blunt the edge of the barbarity itself. In fact, by rendering the rape purely in political terms the writer may end up presenting it to the reader in much the same way as the assailants present it to their victim - as a merely symbolic act. "We're not doing this to you, but your father," they tell her (p. 119): Amina is regarded simply as an attribute of her father and becomes, metonymically, what the attribute stands for. What is disturbing about the fantasy-ridden politics of characters like Medina and Sagal (and Koschin in the earlier novel) is that they appear to partake of the totalitarian state's frightening capacity for making a nominal reality prevail over the actual; for giving the symbolic or representative signifier priority over its referent and, in the process, promoting principle irrelevantly over particulars, ideology over instance. Medina proliferates metonymic motifs regardless of fitness or occasion, culminating in the gigantic solipsism which indexes her house arrest to the condition of the state and her rearrangement of the furniture in her room to the shaking, "with seismic determination," of the foundations of the national house of Somalia. The same tendency is present in the wilful official fiction that a sixteen-year-old American-born daughter of Somali expatriates on her first trip, as a tourist, to her ancestral home is really a Somali citizen on whose person the state has licence to perform a brutal circumcision. Things must first be themselves before they can be made into symbols; they must be experienced before the "meaning" is abstracted. Perhaps with this in mind, Farah, without dwelling upon the lurid details, makes the two barbarities suitably savage and shocking.

This extrapolative habit of mind is most advanced and most acutely felt in the character of Medina. In *Sardines* we are aware, as with Loyaan's reassembling of Soyaan's life in the previous book, of minds self-consciously engaged in the quasi-fictional reconstruction of reality after the event. It is another of Farah's novels of discourse and debate (with Medina as a more serious, female Koschin), written at an intellectual distance from and on a theoretic slant to events. Sagal, notes Medina, is much given to "inventing futures for herself" (p. 128), while in the psychology of her mentor fluidity and fixation paradoxically mingle. On the one hand, it is Medina's habit to fictionalize her own past and reconstruct a multiplicity of possible motives for her actions, none of which is apparently to be preferred above the others, and she is abetted in this by the plurality of oral versions of her doings (notably, her abandonment of Samater) which are rumoured into circulation hot on the heels of the event. Delighting in her existential doubts, Medina appropriates others' versions of her own actions (Sagal's, Nasser's) as is convenient (pp. 63, 82). The flexibility, however, is born of fixation. Medina is the bookish intellect caged by political repression, struggling desperately to construct its own human reality to rival the political unreality outside but in the process driven paranoically in upon itself to the point where it identifies the personal with the political and starts to mistake its own fictional reconstructions for fact.

Placed under a banning order and effective house arrest, Medina writes herself out of the public, political world and into a private, fictional world, where she has but a single disciple, her protege Sagal, and a captive audience of one, her daughter Ubax. From the boundaried isolation of a room in her brother's house - "In Medina's mind the world was reduced to a room" (p. 24) - Medina proceeds imaginatively to restructure the world in the light of a few narrow principles:

> She reconstructed the story from the beginning. She worked it into a set of pyramids which served as foundations for one another. Out of this, she erected a construction of great solidity and strength. She then built mansions on top of it all, mansions as large as her imagination and with lots of chambers that led off corridors in which she lost herself. [...] She roamed about in the architecture of her thoughts. (p. 2)

If the house is Medina's life - "a life defined like the boundaries of a property" (p. 6) - and the room her mind, in which her thoughts walk up and down unhindered, its spaces are the blank pages on which will be constructed her book criticizing the revolution (*this* book, in effect, since her consciousness occupies the largest space in it), and the furniture signifies whatever inconveniences distract the writer from her obsession: "one's mind bumped into things, was distracted by the material things around" (p. 17). It is all, in reality, a massive projection of the subjective will which at the end claims immoderately to have shaken the pillars of state and rendered her an active participant in its history. The room is, finally, a reductive metaphor for the intransigent idealist's and self-absorbed novelist *manque's* selfish rearrangement of others' lives, as if they were merely the furniture of her own brain, and of her own life in a way that is heedless of the effects upon others who come into contact with it:

> Medina has changed the position of a chair. That is all. She has created a habitat in which she alone can function, she has created a condition in which she alone can live. No room for either Samater or Ubax. How has she done this? She put the chair in the wrong place in the dark. When Samater awoke he stumbled on it and broke his neck. (p. 243)

Whatever its errors and limitations, however, Medina's typifying, ideologizing approach to character and event serves an important purpose in the novel in that it explicitly formulates, albeit less subtly than in *Sweet and Sour Milk*, the links between parental and political tyranny. In *Sardines* the doctrinal axioms fly fast and furious: "Power as a system, power as a function. [...] The sky would fall in on anyone who upset a pillar of society - in this case Idil" (Medina, p. 52); "In an authoritarian state, the head of the family (matriarch or patriarch) plays a necessary and strong role; he or she represents the authority of the state" (Sagal, p. 62); "There is one thing society will not forgive him: for disobeying the authority of an aged mother. Idil represents traditional authority, and it is in the old and not the young that society invests power" (Samater, p. 23). The power system which is built into the Somali social fabric, and of which the General is merely a manifestation, is as evident in the passive powers of the matriarch - the right to be listened to and obeyed, the right to profit from her son's prosperity and not to be ejected from his house - as it is in the active ones of the patriarch, and political pressure will be brought to bear upon any member of the family who breaks with tradition. But Farah, ever a scrupulously fair writer even at his most partisan, allows even the terrible Idil to have her say and is sufficiently generous to give her an existence beyond the political stereotype. Monster though she may be to the Western mind, her grasping materialism is made comprehensible in the context of her history of poverty and privation, and her responses to the Western challenge to her kind of civilisation at least score more points than Keynaan's in the previous book:

> I am what and who I am. I am the product of a tradition with a given coherence and solidity; you, of confusion and indecision. [...] What is more, your generation hasn't produced the genius who could work out and develop an alternative cultural philosophy acceptable to all the members of your rank and file; no genius to propose something with which you could replace what you've rejected. (pp. 77-78)

Idil cannot reasonably be expected to cast off her Islamic faith for a secular alternative or accept a son who cooks and lives off his wife's wealth in his wife's house. In the New Year Festival that keeps appearing in the background of the novel, the corpse of the slaughtered year, representing the senile old age institutionally invested with power by the regime, must be allowed to burn itself to ash before the youthful fires of renewal can be lit. "Years begin with the rekindling of a new fire and the extinguishing of the old," muses Medina (p. 132), though in *Sardines* the old consume the young instead of making way for them - "A young fire extinguished [...] and the old not yet!" (p. 110) - and the delay perhaps throws an undue emphasis on continuity and preservation. These also have an importance in the scheme of things, however, and Farah does not allow them to go unnoticed. The regime may not, in the end, be a monstrous aberration from Somali traditions since those traditions are at least better able to cope with dictatorship than the habits of Western individualism ("Tradition stays and wins in the end," warns Idil). They are also, through the extended family's group economics and imperatives of hospitality and assistance, better equipped to deal with the crises of famine and refugees, though at a cost to privacy and property rights which Samater - and perhaps Farah himself - finds unacceptably high.

The same complementarity and antinomy attend the analogic motifs - rooms and furniture, clocks and currents, lizards and beached whales, two as "a number of possible contraries" - which weave a baroque course across this most poetically intense and intricate of novels. Even the broadly archetypal, elementalising typology taken by Fatima from the Arab tradition (in which Medina is fire and pillar, Nasser water, and Samater/shimbir the bird) is full of ambivalences. The metaphor of Promethean fire that envelops Medina makes her the harbinger of enlightenment, the founder of a new order, and links her with Hindu myths in which women created fire. But the latter allusion also triggers negative associations with the Hindu practice of suttee and with the story of the woman who accidentally sets fire to her hut and burns her child (as Medina burns her own child with the fires of precocious knowledge and freedom). The prevalent symbolism of the annual purification ceremony of the Fire Festival in the second part of the novel refers not only to the moribund nature of the regime. It also enshrouds Medina with an ironic tropology of burnt-out husks, smouldering embers and ash, which are suggestive of both her prematurely extinguished energies and the devastating effects of her incendiary behaviour (her mother refers to her as "the fire which nearly burned everything at birth"; p. 135). Additionally, fire, like water, blurs the vision and fosters illusion. Medina's ideological ardour fuels fantasies of power and liberation which flicker and fade in the more realistic presence of her mother: "The fire in her eyes died, so did the flame of her fantasies" (p. 135).

As with fire, so with water. This is the element of the schoolgirl swimming champion Sagal, who is associated throughout with moving currents and bridges to the future: Medina is imaged as a structure, Sagal as a process. Sagal, as water, signifies promise and potentiality: Wentworth George tells her that the Somali word for both water and sperm, "biyo," is the same as the Greek word for life, "bio" (p. 230). But she is also the epitome of transience and irresolution, her life changed whimsically by every passing current of experience and forever prey to the unexpected and incalculable: she "would swim in the pools of an unplanned future" (p. 57) and, falling pregnant, feels "exposed like the rain which catches one unprepared" (p. 225) (even then, she is not certain that she *is* pregnant). Amina says of her: "Sagal is a river changing course, country, beds, master and lover" (p. 26). The liquid element connotes also the blur and rust of unreality - "Water forms rust, water makes things go rotten" (p. 26) - and these in Sagal are the marks of a hyper-active, over-inventive imagination, always "wearing a watery grin, squinting slightly" at an imperceptive angle to reality (p. 44). She is described, significantly, as "a skimmer of a swimmer" (p. 26), one who moves along the surface of reality without penetrating it. But the only way that she can cross the waters to the world of freedom and new experience beckoning to her from Europe is to plunge into them, to win the national championship and have her fame rewarded with foreign travel. The alternative is to follow her mother's advice, to stay at home and have her child, thus exchanging her fluid, unstable element for the procreative native earth: "The earth is warm when a seed is buried in it," Ebla tells her, "and a mother is happy when there is a child in her" (p. 224). The elements of water, fire and earth are, moreover, not exclusive but continuous and complementary forces, alike in their ambivalent combination of life-giving and destructive powers, and Farah is fond of entwining them in his typology. Thus, for example, in Medina's dream of her mother-in-law's death, the desert nomad Idil appears, strangely, as a huge floating whale "buried in the secret womb of the sea" (p. 196), while Fatima, the Yemeni woman from across the Red Sea, proffers a "dry hand" to the kisses of young female visitors. When Ebla and Sagal walk out into the night "like two feathered doves," the motifs of earth-mother and river-daughter, land and current, dryness and deluge, are ingeniously combined in "an image as fascinating as the whirlpool of a herdsman's dust" (p. 35).[12]

Farah rings most of the changes, however, on the pervasive house-room-chairs complex of motifs which I have already touched upon. These radiate out in a series of concentric circles from the human brain, in which Medina's thoughts freely perambulate, to the "room of one's own [...] a room (and a century) in which one was not a guest" (p. 3), a separate inner space where patriarchy, matriarchy and the regime's power have no place. They expand from the claustrophobic domestic space in which Somali women are confined to the national house of Somalia overrun by Soviet "white ants"; and finally, a few pages from the end, they contract from Medina's ideal "city of righteousness" to the bare room which, as we have seen, serves as a metaphor for her rearrangement of the lives around her. In the course of these widening and shrinking spirals the motifs gather a fair weight of irony. Perhaps one of the "bombs that explode in the face of the reader", to use Medina's phrase for good writing, is the telling tirade of accusations by Xaddia in the Epilogue, which explode "like a bombshell in Medina's ears" (p. 246) and give a hollow ring to her closing claim that the rebuilding of her private world has caused tremors in the state.

Sardines marks an interesting point in the progress of Farah's thinking about the oral tradition. Although the General poses hypocritically as another word-bringing Prophet, his power is still an oral-based one that lives in awe and apprehension of the written word. "The power of the written word is immense," Sagal comments on the dawn-daubings, relishing the irony of the General's Prospero-like provision of an orthography to curse him in. Banning orders compulsorily oralize literature: Medina is forbidden to publish her translations of world classics from six languages, so she serves them up, oral-fresh, as a domestic diet of bedtime stories for Ubax, an audience of one. Communications with the world outside the house are possible only on an oral basis: in keeping with the Somali proverb that "what is seen by more than four eyes is considered of public knowledge and what is heard by more than two ears is no longer a secret" (p. 49), that world is governed by gossip, libellous rumour and speculation which sustain the atmosphere of suspicion and insecurity, of being "kept guessing", required by the dictator. A Somali poet observes that the ear, the organ of both the oral culture and the General's police system, is shaped like a question-mark, and Amina and Sagal exchange looks "with question-marks like pendant earrings" (pp. 170, 236). In this unhealthy, hothouse atmosphere, rumour becomes a kind of contagion. Sagal's attempted boycott of the swimming competition is attended by swarms of eavesdropping informers, "rumour-carriers" who "spread the word the way filthy air scatters germs and disease" (p. 229). Medina's clanswomen, all creatures of the oral code, "live in the innards of a whale which hardly went ashore", encaged in the watery unreality of rumour and hearsay. No sooner has Medina made her decisive move from home when a number of versions of the event are already in circulation and on their way back to her, presenting her with a variety of possible reasons for her action: Idil's threat to have Ubax circumcised; the compromising of her anti-government position by Samater's ministerial appointment; Samater's rumoured infidelity with the maid; the creation of a need for herself through absence (a variation on the General's "starve and rule" policy); and the desire to bring about a confrontation between Samater and Idil. Medina is either unwilling or unable to confirm which of these, if any, is the correct one. The oral convention thus poses not merely a moral usurpation and an invasion of private sanctities, but also an ontological threat, since it takes the personal reality of individuals out of their hands and makes it a public property. Private certainty is dissolved into public indeterminacy, singleness of motive rumoured into multiplicity, until the agent of the act is herself left doubtful of her own motive. The oral code's multiplication of possibilities acquaints people with their own inner uncertainties about who (or even *if*) they are, thus undermining their sense of self and posing an existential threat to their very being. Of another group of women, from another culture, who suffered under an obscurantist dictatorship, the Chinese author Jung Chang has written:

> Under a dictatorship like Mao's, where information was withheld and fabricated, it was very difficult for ordinary people to have confidence in their own experience or knowledge. [...] The whole nation slid into doublespeak. Words became divorced from reality, responsibility, and people's real thoughts. Lies were told with ease because words had lost their meanings - and had ceased to be taken seriously by others.[13]

Something very similar to this is seen happening to the Somali women in *Sardines*. As in the previous novel, the oral tradition in *Sardines* is allied to the forces of authoritarian reaction and obscurantism, personified here in the uneducated, illiterate Idil, in whose oral world mental and cultural nomadism join hands:

> And by the time you were ready to ask her a question, you would discover that she had already moved on, taking refuge in unscientific generalizations;

> you would find that she had changed residence and had nomaded away, impermanent as Fatima bint Thabit was permanent in her fixed abode. (p. 7)

Enshrined in power, Idil has no need of rational defences and her mind butterflies off, merely touching upon arguments it is unable to sustain and preferring the pluralist, many-versioned form of reality which she can more easily mould into the shape of her own obsessive vision: "Idil's ball of thread rolled away. [...] She then began to thread-draw in her mind a past with patterns different from the one she had the intention of re- narrating" (p. 78). None of this is new, merely recapitulating and expanding upon ideas introduced in *Sweet and Sour Milk*.

What is new in *Sardines* is the attention paid to the radical wing of the oral tradition. Medina herself, who classes Somalis as "non-bookly", takes no special cognizance of Somali poets, absorbing their psalms to their daughters and such gestures of hope for the future into the mainstream of world literature alongside Yeats and Tagore. But we are introduced, through Medina's brother Nasser, to Dulman, the legendary singer glimpsed in the last movement of *A Naked Needle* whose songs, exploited by the Revolutionary Council's propaganda machine, earned her the official title "Lady of the Revolution." Dulman has now defected and thrown in her lot with the struggle against the regime by smuggling underground tapes of subversive poems, recorded straight from the poet's mouth, then learned and worked into unscripted theatrical pieces for outside performance. In this barely literate but vivid and eloquent woman, Farah presents an image of an ancient oral Somalia, a guest in a century of high-technology which it must turn to its own account if it is to survive: "It takes ages and a great deal of patience to become a literate people. [...] At my age it isn't easy to adapt to new things" (pp. 160-61). But adapt she does, for the country's oral artistic traditions are not burnt out but retain an extraordinary vitality and a potentially revolutionary energy. "Our tradition is oral, " she insists. "One can communicate with the hearts of Somalis only through their hearing faculties" (p. 170). Cassettes are the tradition's answer to the debased oral techniques that keep the General in power; they are the means by which it strikes a response and refuses submission, so that written literature is no longer a lone threat to despotism. It is significant that the slogan-painting girls sign themselves 'Dulman.' The generic meaning of the word is 'victim' and, since the graffiti-artists are women, it can be taken to refer to the whole of victimized Somali womanhood. But it appears also to include a personal reference to the legendary "Lady of the Revolution" (a revolution long betrayed) who is now identified with the struggle against dictatorship. "The power of the written word is immense," says Amina (p. 125) but, as in the first novel of the trilogy, it is not sufficient by itself alone. In *Sardines* the voices of protest are now combined: the power of the spoken word is joined to that of the written one.

CHAPTER SIX
The Grandfather: *Close Sesame*

After the focus on various modes of matriarchy in *Sardines*, Farah closes his trilogy with a last look at the patriarchy and, perhaps to redress the balance of the first two books, presents what is a unique specimen in his writing: a patriarch who is not a tyrant. Up to this point in the trilogy the patriarchal model has been the brutal, grotesque Keynaan - paternalism in its most destructive, life-denying form. But in Deeriye, the protagonist of *Close Sesame*, Farah gives us patriarchy with a human face and his most endearing hero. The familiar doubling of children and parents couples in this work the two sons, Mursal and Mukhtaar, and their respective fathers. Mukhtaar's father, Sheikh Ibrahim, is the prototypical "Grand Patriarch" who, in a blaze of rage and wrath fanned by the General, takes the life that he has given. By contrast, Mursal's father Deeriye is a gentle, sage and saintly figure (his name means "the one who offers warmth"). A devout Muslim and traditional Somali, Deeriye is a loving monogamous husband still mourning his dead wife, and a beloved father and grandfather who lives harmoniously with children and grandchildren in a non-authoritarian household. He is also a veteran and national hero of resistance to the Italians during the colonial period and an outspoken opponent of the General's regime: a man who has spent twelve years of his life in detention, eight of them in colonial prisons and more recently, as a result of his criticisms of the General's public execution of opponents, another four in independence jails. His own period of political activism and persecution, however, lies in the past. Old and ill, subject to asthmatic fits of a frightening intensity, he is now taken care of by his children: first by his doctor daughter Zeinab and then, when house renovations threaten his peace, by his son Mursal, a law professor, and Mursal's Jewish American wife Natasha. In his son's house Deeriye is subject only to the loving pressures of a benevolent domestic authoritarianism; he submits to the little tyrannies of tenderness that pester him, over-protectively, with anxious solicitations about his health and medical regimen.

Meanwhile, in the public domain the political tyranny of military rule continues unabated. The regime has switched from Soviet to Western sponsorship, though this makes little difference to its politics, which are still based on a clan system dating back to nomadic times: both the old and new alignments are merely marriages of convenience that involve only superficial imitations of the super-powers' ideologies. To appease foreign observers and aid donors from Western democracies, the General puts on a farcical rigged election in which there are separate ballot boxes: a "Yes" box draped with the Somali flag and a "No" box marked "For Enemies of the Nation," the latter menacingly invigilated by the security police (for "Nation," read the General's ruling clan). Active opposition to the dictatorship continues to be carried out by the younger generation, with the same ineffectual results (though the gestural protest of *Sardines* has here graduated to full conspiracy), and it is into the ranks of this opposition that Deeriye's son is drawn. "After you and me," says Medina to Samater at the end of the previous book, "it is Mursal and Mahad's turn."[1] These two are joined in the third part of the trilogy by Mukhtaar, a member of the General's own clan, and an ex-army officer Jibriil. Mahad is imprisoned and tortured after a kamikaze attempt on the life of the General, who then manipulates the clan network so as to suggest that the abortive strike was the tribally-motivated act of a lone madman acting on a momentary impulse, thus denying it any nationalistic dimension or ideological grounding. The regime's well-tried trick is to "call the nationalist tribalist and the tribalist nationalist": the first is what it calls its opponents, the second what it calls itself. The General next proceeds to isolate both the assailant and his family by prevailing upon the clan, under threat of a general purge, to excommunicate both Mahad and his adoptive father Rooble, a close friend of Deeriye. Although Mahad has not betrayed any of his confederates, Mukhtaar is implicated by association, and when his involvement becomes known it poses problems for the General: firstly, because the revolt would assume nationalist proportions and an air of concerted organization if it were admitted that more than one clan was involved; secondly, because Mukhtaar is of his own tribal group and is, in the words of the informant Afrah, "the water the General's own clan has choked on."[2] Unable to disgrace his own clan by taking any public, official action against his kinsman, the dictator has his tribal elders decree that the matter be settled within the family, by which it is understood that Sheikh Ibrahim, a staunch supporter of the regime, is to kill his son.[3] This he does, though not at the first attempt. After his father has tried to club him to death, Mukhtaar appears on Deeriye's doorstep, wounded, dishevelled and apparently mad. There is then a second fight during which Mukhtaar dies but this, like most of the action in *Close Sesame*, takes place off-stage, so exactly what happens is not clear. An official verdict of suicide is pronounced by Ahmed-Wellie, the suspicious spy-doctor of *Sweet and*

Sour Milk and now the Minister of Information, and as Ahmed-Wellie appears to have been present at the death, there is a suggestion that he may have helped to hasten Mahad's exit. Jibriil is the next to go, killed in a bungled bomb-plot, and finally Mursal himself, the intellectual driving force of the conspiracy, is picked up by the security police. Shortly afterwards the unofficial news reaches Deeriye and his family that Mursal has died in prison, his death already portended by the playing of the funeral dirge, the *Samadiidow*, on the national radio. Though an ailing asthmatic veteran and by nature a man of peace who has always eschewed violence, Deeriye decides to take the *lex talionis* into his own hands and avenge his son's murder. His own climactic assassination attempt on the life of the dictator fails, like all the others, and he dies on a military parade ground in a hail of machine-gun bullets. At the end of the trilogy the General's hold on power is as strong as ever and, apart from Medina, all the members of the Group of Ten which began with Soyaan are dead, imprisoned or exiled. The movement has failed absolutely - which is not surprising, considering that it has made no attempt to expand beyond the bounds of the "privilegentzia" and build a broad popular front by recruiting members from the rank and file. Its methods, moreover, have remained as confused as its motives. Though Farah continues to insist on the value and necessity of political commitment, he demonstrates in this third novel that actions by inept lone assassins, easily isolated and targeted by the security police, are no more effectual, and no less futile, than subversion from within the ruling establishment in the first book and passive resistance from without in the second.

The foregoing, like most plot summaries, makes the issues and subject-matter of the novel sound deceptively clear-cut: in fact, *Close Sesame* is one of the most elusive, recondite and unresolved of Farah's fictions. The author has said in an interview that he associates open-ended narratives and multiple viewpoints with freedom and tolerance, closure and the single omniscient view with tyranny (dictators insist that there is only one way of looking at things): "I usually doubt almost everything, and therefore, because I doubt, I would look at different possibilities of looking at the same thing."[4] In this he is echoed by Deeriye in the novel: "It is the prerogative of God alone to be sure of anything. I am only a human. And therefore I am in doubt" (p. 202). Its menacing title notwithstanding, *Close Sesame* is not about closure, except in the most limited political sense: in Africa national liberation closes the door on individual freedoms, independence produces tyranny. Far from sealing away mythical wealth of the kind conjured up by the reference to Ali Baba's cave, Farah's narrative opens up, through the memory and personality of Deeriye, a rich cultural treasure trove of esoteric Koranic lore, protean oral legend, obscure Islamic and little-known Somali history, all fertile with allusion and multiple in suggestiveness. In fact, at times perhaps too much light is admitted to the cave, in beams of too many colours, falling at a confusing number of angles. Deeriye's is a "life resplendent with contradictions," frought with "the tensions of a complicated set of polarities" (p. 159). Subsequently, the ambiguous and paradoxical, the unexplained and indeterminate, occupy so much space in his narrative that it is uncertain whether the final effect is a polyvalency of meaning or a massive aporia at the core of the book.

To begin with, the novel's mode of narration is elliptical and indirect as a result of the effect on the narrative viewpoint of the protagonist's physical frailty and ailing condition. Deeriye drifts in and out of consciousness, nodding off to sleep in conversations and political meetings and often unable to distinguish what he has heard from what he has dreamed in his frequent cat-naps and daydreams or seen in the visions that precede his asthmatic seizures. He is at a distance from the world around him, out of touch with and only fitfully observant of it, his perception of reality filtered intermittently through rumours and intuitions as much as through reports and observations. Deeriye's life is, as he explains, "landmarked by absences." The exhausted asthmatic is mentally absent from his present life as the imprisoned political martyr was physically absent from his past one, though this absent-minded distraction may prove as much a source of strength as his earlier corporeal absence. As a father Deeriye was an indelible absence, missing from the family photographs and ignorant of his offspring's childhoods, which he has to dream, imagine or learn of second-hand from his brother-in-law. But absence, of course, implies presence, since an absence in one place is a presence in another, a departure here an arrival somewhere else, an act of omission one of commission at another level (as, in the present, Deeriye's omission of a significant word from a Koranic prayer-verse leads, in his own view, to his visions being temporarily withheld).[5] The imprisonment which absented Deeriye from his personal life in the past has given him a very public presence in the here and now, turning him into a living legend whom young hero-worshipping disciples approach on the street to express their reverence and admiration. He has become - albeit at some cost to his privacy - a historical personality and mythic figure, a national celebrity whose life is no longer his own but the property of the community:

> *He* was not a physical person so much as an abstraction: a man whose absence was noted on the printed photograph. *He* was an idea; he was a national *notion. He* was, come to think of it, more than anything else an image; "He became what you wanted," Mahad had said [...] (pp. 14-15)

Deeriye is, in his own words, "a collage of many notions," constituted - whether in the domestic household, the neighbourhood or the clan - from the opinions of other people who refer to him in his presence in the third person, as "*He*," as if he were not there. Each of these proceeds to construct Deeriye in different ways: as a rallying point for sacrificial martyrdom (Mahad); as a springboard for ideas and a symbol of hope for resistance to tyranny (Mursal); as a medical case, to be kept in an allergens-sealed environment (Zeinab); and as a devout and saintly friend and in-law (Rooble, Elmi-Tiir). More importantly, Deeriye's past absences were a source not only of political but also of spiritual power. It was during his colonial imprisonment, alone in his cell with the Koran, that there occurred the religious visions which were to mould his life; here also that there developed the occult spiritual communion with his wife Nadiifa and the extra-sensory, premonitory powers which allowed him to breach the prison walls and know about intimate things that had happened in his family during his absence.

And if Deeriye's past absences have the force and power of presences, then so too do his contemporary ones, for this supra-rational communication has continued into the present: as Deeriye visited Nadiifa during *his* absence, she now visits him, posthumously, during *hers*. In his waking reveries and the fits of abstraction which he refers to as his "memory holes," his late wife counsels him on his relations with his children and grandchildren; grants him the gift of foresight that allows him to predict his stoning by the street urchin Yassin; and, in his last vision, helps him reach a decision about his ultimate course of action. Thus the protagonist, and the action, of *Close Sesame*, are not entirely of this world. Deeriye lives, and much of the novel takes place, in a twilit half-world between sleep and waking, the time between dark and dawn when his dead wife comes visiting. The narrative is situated in a transitional zone between different kinds of truth, on the boundary dividing different orders of reality, featuring phenomena that are simultaneously present and absent, dark in one order and light in another (the book abounds with images of doors, portcullises and drawbridges that prohibit and then admit access, whether to friends and family, knowledge and history, or greater freedoms and concomitant invasions of privacy). In the few seconds before his seizures, Deeriye "crosses over into a world whose logic is unknown to any living soul," and subsequently finds himself "living with different realities"; he is caught between two duelling value systems - his "two selves, two souls," as Nadiifa tells him in her final visitaton - and is "not sure of anything any more" (pp. 116, 143, 198). Those who *are* sure, the doctor daughter and lawyer son, are allowed to have their sceptical, scientific-rationalist say about their father's visions, and Farah himself, in an interview statement, has made some attempt to resolve the conflict by viewing Deeriye's illness as a refuge from public life and commitment, with the inevitable negative political implications that follow from this: "Asthma is a symbol of that enclosure of refusing, in view of old age and the political situation, to come out and be free."[6] But a purely political reading, or a reading in any single reductive set of terms, is unlikely to do justice to the complexities of a novel in which the natural and supernatural, the secular and sacred, rub shoulders. By an inverse proportion, Deeriye's shortage of breath, his failure of exhalative power in the physical world, denotes a corresponding enhanced inhalation of spiritual power in his visionary realm. He is inspired, in the most literal sense of the word, by the breath of Allah in the form of his sacred text the Koran, the name of which derives from the Arabic for "recite"[7] and which, in the novel, is seldom read and is most frequently spoken (in prayer) or heard (on tape). The Divine Word, whether or not it be an empowering agent, is perceived as an oral power, inhaled by devout departing souls who no longer have breath for this life. "In my lungs is my soul," Deeriye is reminded by Nadiifa when the end is near (p. 206), and the book's pervasive Islamic image-complex of breath, chants, ears and lungs - which also stresses Islam's link with oral tradition - keeps open the religious options of the asthma symbol. Certainly, there is no attempt to read Deeriye's illness, in negative material terms, as an evasion of political defeat and a retreat into a private religious quietism, or to write off his problematic spirituality as the psychosomatic product of his bodily illness or his political despair.

The repeated references in the novel to Deeriye's twilit visage - "half in light and half in shadow," engulfed by "dark and white stripes" (pp. 129, 171) - deliberately echo the first description of the civil-servant-turned-itinerant-lunatic Khaliif, "the madman who strode out of dawn's greyness, half his face painted white and the other half dark" (p. 16). Khaliif is the protagonist's automatic analogue. The inspired visionary madman also straddles, liminally, the religious and political, spiritual and temporal worlds, drawing upon the Koran to denounce the crimes and corruptions of the regime and its supporters; and, like Deeriye, he is stoned by the urchin Yassin for speaking truth to the worshippers of false political gods. Only dogs, crows and madmen are stoned by Somalis, but under the dictatorship it is only madmen who dare proclaim the truth in public, thus turning themselves into spokesmen by uttering what everyone has suppressed. By his final suicidal action Deeriye follows Mahad and Jibriil into the ranks of the politically mad and he is, appropriately, rumoured to have spent his last hours wandering in the company of Khaliif. He reflects on the mad mind:

> A mind so overcrowded with ideas and things, a mind made into the symbol of disorder and indecision by the powers that be, a mind rendered useless because it cannot decipher these symbols, cannot tell apart the good shadows from the bad, cannot distinguish between the virtuous and the wicked. [...] For where there is harmony, the regime brings about disharmony; where there is fraternity, the regime brings about death, disorder and disaster [...]. To speak of that about which others are silent and to remain sane at the same time is a very difficult task. I have been on the fringe of *madness* the past forty years: the *madness* of which I talk is in itself a political statement. (pp. 108, 200)

In *Close Sesame* madness is essentially a politically manufactured phenomenon and a measure of political despair. Yet, precisely because of the political context that conditions and determines it, it is hard to define. As Farah has said in an interview, political frustration drives people, irrationally, to "desperate, almost kamikaze acts of bravado" to achieve change[8] or, as Mursal puts it, to "the outrage of the insane" (p. 109). In any case, to cross clan frontiers in a fanatically clannish society is, by the definitions of this society, effectively to cross the line between sanity and madness. The General labels his tribe-transcending rebels "mad" in much the same way as did the Italians Deeriye's act of nationalist defiance and the British the Sayyid, whom they called "the mad mullah" (one definition of a hero in the novel is "a successful madman"). After one of Khaliif's denunciatory tirades a young girl tells the gathered crowd the story of the African dictator who committed the director of a mental hospital to his own institution for siding with the one patient who, after being certified sane, refused to sing the dictator's praise-songs.

Khaliif's madness is, immediately, politically induced, apparently the result of drugs administered during detention, but at the behest of a regime which itself hovers between madness and sanity and regularly strays beyond the bounds of reason in its eagerness to foster madness among its subjects.

Khaliif, Deeriye ponders, is not at home in the world of the sane, "but neither did he belong in the world of the insane for he did not always behave as though he were mad" (p. 17). Though virtually autistic in his self-communings, Khaliif is coolly methodical in the manner in which he targets the houses of stooges of the regime and in his three bizarre rampages he dresses deliberately in the robes of a priest, the uniform of the General and the clothes of the dead Mursal, suggesting a calculated assault beneath a facade of insanity. Deeriye speculates that Mahad's assassination attempt is, similarly, "a premeditated act of madness," meaning that it was really not mad at all but was merely made to look like one man's private lunacy so as to avert suspicion of a concerted conspiracy. The irony is that the conspirators, in striving to give the erratic, haphazard impression of "insanity," come perilously close to the thing itself as regards their methods, for in their eagerness to create an effect they recklessly lower their chances of success. Deeriye sees it as "a sign of maturity" that the four young men "can work in total ignorance of the motives and actions of one another" (p. 112). A more practical revolutionary strategist might reply that the degree of deliberate disorganization is itself taken to lunatic proportions. The three assassination attempts, and the whole issue of what madness is and how, if at all, it can be avoided in a madness-creating society, are left open to rival interpretations. People, says Deeriye, "describe all unexplained mysteries and powers as signs of madness" (p. 50). Madness is another of the novel's numerous aporias, a subject from which explanation is absent.

In the case of Khaliif, the mystery is compounded by interference from Islamic and oral traditions in which the madman is conceived as a channel for the expression of visionary and religious experience. "In Islam madness occupies a mystical position," Farah has said, quoting the Arabic proverb, "all people who receive wisdom from the mouths of the mad remain sane."[9] We see ourselves in the mad, as Deeriye sees himself in Khaliif, and they therefore act as mirrors and touchstones for the sane. Additionally, Somali historians have remarked that some of the best poets in their country's oral tradition are drawn from the class of inspired religious madmen, the "shiikhs, mullahs and mystics"[10] - the divinely inspired illuminati whose minds have been touched by God and who are thought mad only by those who are too deeply immersed in the daily insanities of the material world to recognize higher truths. Khaliif, significantly, unleashes his vitriolic abuse at dawn and dusk, the transitional periods when the oral poet, in vituperative vein, casts his curse, the *cir-gaduud,* upon those who have wronged him, including his political enemies.[11] In directing this traditional feature at the General's regime, Farah may appear to be turning the oral mode to unduly radical effect but, as was made clear in the Introduction to this book, poets in Somalia have always been very public, controversial figures and seminal forces in the influencing of political opinion. Deeriye is a living reminder of this radical oral tradition that fostered the talents of the warrior-poet the Sayyid and the Sultan Wiil-Waal, men who fought colonial and clan enemies with the power of the spoken word as well as with conventional weapons. Though drawn from a misty, quasi-legendary past, the tales of King Wiil-Waal that Deeriye narrates to his grandson Samawade pose challenging, ever-topical questions about the relationship of madness and heroism; the nature of kingship and wisdom (seen not to be the special preserve of rulers); and the optimum conditions for the preservation of peace, of which the even distribution of the society's wealth is the most important.[12] And yet the oral tradition, as the earlier volumes of the trilogy have demonstrated, is a double-edged sword, with Dulman as one blade and "Dionysius's Ear" as the other. In his dawn rampages the madman Khaliif, portentously, plays various and often opposing roles, denouncing first the traitorous house of Cigaal and then, in a parody of the dictator, Deeriye's own house. Moreover, the Sayyid, whose poems feed Deeriye's Pan-Somali optimism and revolutionary ardour, inspired both devotion and terror in his people, and his revolution was nationalistic rather than social; while Wiil-Waal was a ruthless and absolute, albeit an enlightened and benevolent, dictator.[13]

The name Khaliif also receives some impetus from the Islamic *Khalifah*, the intermediary or vicegerent of God who embodies, theomorphically, the God-like in man, the something in him which aspires to divinity[14] (Deeriye "misses the presence of God in himself" when his own spiritual intermediary, Nadiifa, fails to visit). Finally, Deeriye reminds us that the Somalis stone crows as well as dogs and madmen, and that the crow, because its "*waaq*" is the Somali word for God, was once worshipped, thus loosely attaching another sacred dimension to Khaliif's character. Thus Farah surrounds his mystery madman with a confusing superabundance of allusions and at one particular recondite reversal the reader may suspect the author of gratuitous mystification. This is when he gives to the urchin who casts stones at Deeriye and Khaliif the name of the holy messenger who in the 36th Sura of the Koran brings the word of the Lord to the unbelievers of Antioch and is himself threatened with stoning (Deeriye dies with a tattered copy of this Koranic chapter in his pocket). Farah's Yassin is the son of Cigaal, the worshipper of a false political god: in Khaliif's words, one of those "upstarts of the worse kind, upstarts who have upturned our sacred traditions and have begun worshipping *him* [...] a mortal and a fool at that in place of Him" (p. 20). Instead of casting stones at Satan as in Islamic tradition, the lapidator is here himself a satanic figure who hurls his missiles with impunity, secure in the protection of the god of power, his vicious behaviour condoned by both family and state. Koranic commentators on the 36th Sura have noted that abbreviated letters *Ya-Sin* are notoriously ambiguous and impossible to be dogmatic about,[15] and Farah's text is in much the same mould. The point of the inversion may be to demonstrate the incompatibility of the Koran with the contemporary political order into which it has been deviously insinuated; or the very retention of the sacred name and its connection with stoning may signify that the light of the higher religious truth still glimmers through its garbled expression, that the Holy Word survives its material corruption since it is not possible to pervert a religion in its entirety.

Of all Farah's novels, *Close Sesame* has the strongest sense of history. Though the events it describes are firmly anchored in the post-1980 Somali Emergency, the book has a long retrospective reach, ranging from the contemporary crisis back to the Italian Fascist occupation and the Dervish War against the British in the first quarter of the century, and further back yet to the semi-legendary past of King Wiil-Waal and the even more remote period of the Islamic Caliphate. For Deeriye the present is measured out in prayers, the past in a series of epochal moments of choice and confrontation which serve as touchstones for the present. In his consciousness contemporary events unfold in patterns parallel to, and in some cases replicas of, happenings of long ago. Jacqueline Bardolph aptly puts it thus:

> History here is not an absurd sequence of chance occurrences, nor a determined concentration of cause and effect which would render moral decisions irrelevant. The novel underlines the idea that there is a latent pattern to history by pointing repeatedly at coincidences, parallels, echoes, facts that through decades seem to refer to one another. One may feel at times that the writer, playing the part of the Omnipotent Creator, accumulates too many coincidences.[16]

Indeed, the last point is well taken. While the present which is still being lived through is all formless chaos and confusion, full of uncertain information and contradictory reports (eg. Mukhtaar's and Deeriye's deaths), the past is perhaps too temptingly analyzable, too easy to label and formulate into patterns. Thus Deeriye, as a Pan-Somalist and Pan-Africanist, is eager to make the military triumph of the Sayyid chime perfectly with the year of both his own birth and that of the Pan-African Congress: to this end, he moves the Sayyid's defeat of Richard Corfield at the Battle of Dulmadobe in August 1913 to 1912.[17] As Bardolph says, "Deeriye's life is deliberately conceived in symbolic terms."[18] It needs to be added, however, that the visionary allegorical mode, achieved by the juggling of dates and other historical sleights-of-hand, is largely the conception of the character and not that of the author, who is careful to qualify the parallels in a number of instances. "Time was history," says Farah's narrator in one of the book's politico-philosophical *longeurs*, "and history consisted of these illuminated prints - not truths [...] history was a congeries of half-truths" (p. 86). History is not a clearcut neutral black-and-white but takes colour from the interpretive light shone upon it, existing only as it is received and patterned in the present.

A special feature of *Close Sesame* is its doubling and even tripling of sequences of events. Most conspicuous among these is a two-way historical parallel which compares Deeriye's wartime resistance of the Italian colonial regime, on the one side, to his opposition to the General's neo-colonial junta in the present and, on the other, to the earlier war waged against the British administration by the Dervish political and religious leader, national hero and poet, Sayyid Muhammad 'Abdille Hassan (known as the Sayyid). Through the pivotal link of Deeriye, the Sayyid's struggles against the British in the early 1900s are also paired indirectly with subversive and incendiary actions against the General in the post-1980 clampdown. Deeriye is imprisoned by both the Italians and the General for political sentiments that are broadly Sayyidist and he is linked to the warrior-poet throughout the novel in a number of ways. Firstly, there is his religious devoutness and his love of the Sayyid's poetry: poetry and Islam have been described as the cornerstones of Somali culture[19] and Deeriye, who like the Sayyid writes in Arabic and communicates orally in Somali, has deep roots in both worlds. Secondly, there is his politics:

Deeriye is "a Pan-Somalist, because a Somali nationalist" (p. 16). He thinks beyond narrow clan issues, gives national unity priority over kinship allegiances and, as a Somali irredentist, places broad ethnic homogeneity above state boundaries. Both Deeriye and his beloved Sayyid attempt to unite Somalis, regardless of tribal, provincial and colonial identity; the latter by his war against the British, the former by persuading his clan to grant political asylum to a fugitive of another clan who has in self-defence killed an Italian: "Aren't we all one clan and aren't the Italians our enemy?" (p. 38).

The detailed comparisons are sometimes sharply illuminating and sometimes, as with the backwards parallel of Deeriye's defiance of the Italians with the Sayyid's exploits, inexact and farfetched; though the past is a current, daily touchstone for urgent choices, its signpostings are often anachronistic and misleading. At times it is the fine details that fail to match up perfectly. For example, the traitor Haji Omer, who betrays Deeriye into the hands of the Italians by intercepting a message and abusing the innocent trust of the eight-year-old messenger, does not bear close comparison with his elected historical prototype, Haji Abdallah Sheheri, who in 1909 (the year of Haji Omer's birth) was used by the Italians to discredit and mildly denounce the Sayyid's Jihaad as a violation of basic Islamic principles. On other occasions it is the broader visions that are at variance and their implied values which are at stake. The modes of resistance employed by Deeriye and the Sayyid, and their respective effects, actually have very little in common. On his desert campaigns the Dervish leader participated intimately in the mass struggles and sufferings of his people, whereas Deeriye is in fact removed from them by his action: for his single act of defiance he goes to jail to suffer individual privations while his people, presumably, starve in the famine wrought in retaliation by the Italian military. "Shaka Zulu, Ataturk, Nkrumah, Garibaldi, Lenin, Cabdunnaasir, Gandhi, the Sayyid," claims Deeriye, "have one thing in common: the shaping force of their lives has been resistance" (p. 147). In fact, the link is a tenuous one. The Sayyid initiated the crusade against the British himself, virtually declaring war on them in a letter denouncing their oppression of Islam. His was therefore the active, aggressive kind of resistance exemplified by Shaka and Garibaldi. Meanwhile, Deeriye, who merely refuses to betray a name and fatalistically endures imprisonment, is one of history's passive resisters; he is a moral rather than a military hero, one who in a dilemma chooses the most difficult option because he believes it to be right, and who therefore belongs more properly with Nkrumah and Gandhi. Deeriye is more martyr than warrior and it is as a martyr that he dies. "A hero must not die an anonymous death," he tells himself, "he must die, like the Sayyid, in the full knowledge of his actions, bearing the consequences" (p. 35). The Sayyid died ill, exhausted by a succession of defeats, but secure in his accomplishments, and though the Dervish movement fell apart after his death in 1921, his brand of nationalism left its mark on Somali life.[20] Deeriye invests his life in the Sayyidist cause but not - at the material level - his death, which, in comparison with his hero's, is a futile and anti-climactic one, suicide rather than death on active service: he fumbles his weapon and is mown down by machine-guns.

The forward-looking parallels between the anti-colonial struggles and contemporary resistance to the General are also a mixed bag. Naturally, Mahad's lonely martyrdom is not meant to stand serious comparison with the successful collective action of the Dervish charge at Dulmadobe, or Deeriye's current doubt and indecision with the Sayyid's unwavering determination and strength of purpose. The parallels are chiefly valuable, rather, for the light they shed on the General's methods and on their continuity with those of the former colonial administrations. Detention opens Deeriye's thoughts up to the "history and contradictions which the neo-colonial person lives in" and to the whole "neo-colonial system" of which he is the product (p. 93). The General employs the same mendacious tricks and subterfuges as the British and Italian colonizers[21] and, like them, rules through the clans and gets them to do his work for him. The *lex talionis* enforced on an absolute basis by the Sayyid, regardless of clan custom, is used by the dictator, as by the colonizers, on a selective, convenience basis, and is suspended altogether for members of his own clan. Moreover, the General, like his colonial precursors, employs a system of tribal infiltration to isolate individuals within, and then excommunicate them from, their clans; unprotected, they can thence be easily hunted down and picked off by his security police and their deaths blamed on tribal in-fighting. To this end, he has the aging Deeriye hauled up before a tribal inquisition for his ideological stand against state power as, in 1897, the young Sayyid was brought before the Qadiriya, the council of tribal elders, to defend his theological position. And he makes much the same use of Haji Omer's son as the Italians made of the father: he sends Omer junior and his two fellow-spies into the meeting of Deeriye's clan to make known his own wishes and thence to turn the clan against his old enemy. And the General, in true neo-colonial fashion, makes the same mistakes and miscalculations as the British and Italians before him, with the result that his plans backfire in like manner. First, he fails to reckon with the prestige and charisma that Deeriye enjoys as folk-hero and colonial martyr at both clan and national levels. Deeriye's clan, unlike Mahad's, refuses to excommunicate him, as it refused fifty years ago to surrender to the Italians the fugitive taken in at Deeriye's request, and responds by ejecting the three stooges sent to execute the General's business. Next, the dictator's more serious mistake is to underestimate the strength of nationalist feeling and to assume that everything can be handled on the kinship level; blinded by his own incestuous tribalism, he is unable to conceive of anything beyond the clan allegiances on which he bases his rule. Deeriye makes two other startling discoveries in his second period of detention, the first of which is that "the same men who served the colonial governments were now serving these dictatorships or authoritarian regimes" (p. 93). Cigaal, a former colonial collaborator, is employed by the regime as an informant, along with the sons of traitors like Omer who betrayed Somali patriots to the Italian police. Indeed, under Barre's regime the poems of the Sayyid were still banned because - such is the inveteracy of ancient clan rivalries - they contained diatribes against families of the dictator's own Mareehaan clan who fifty years earlier had collaborated with the colonial authorities.[22] The other important discovery that Deeriye makes is that the bitter struggles of the colonial past, both the Sayyid's and his own, were much less complicated than those of the neo-colonial present. In the days of the Sayyid the convergence of colonialism and missionary Christianity gave rein to a broadly unified, militantly patriotic brand of Islam which ensured that the foe was clearly defined. By contrast, in the present day the nationalist and true believer finds himself up against an indigenous regime which has hijacked both the clan support system and the Islamic religion for its own perverted purposes. The enemy keeps shifting his ground and is harder to fight.

Another function of the network of historical parallels is to explore the causative roles of fathers in the lives of their sons and the extent to which the past is not only a reference point for but also a determinant of the future. "Like father, like son" appears to be only one of the possible permutations here for, though history repeats itself in the present, it does so, as the book's title suggests, with some variations and a few outright reversals. The young Omer is clearly no better than his father and the illegitimate son of the evil colonial quisling Cigaal is already, at the age of eight, a vicious thug. Mukhtaar, however, nurtures ideals of brotherhood and nation - ideals he dies for - that are quite independent of his family and totally opposed to the fanatically clannish, patriarchal views of his father. It transpires, meanwhile, that Mahad is only Rooble's nephew and adopted son. He is actually the son of the fugitive sheltered by Deeriye's clan, and the parallels between past and present are again intricately interwoven. The father wrestles a colonial policeman for possession of his gun and accidentally kills him; fifty years on the son wrestles a bodyguard's revolver out of its holster to assassinate a neo-colonial dictator; and in almost the same moment that Mahad junior fails to kill the General, the son of the General's local informant almost succeeds in killing Deeriye, the rescuer of Mahad senior. History comes full circle and seems to be locked into a wheel of repetition, a cyclic determinism from which there is no escape. A circular course is also charted across the narrative by the motifs of intercepted, distorted and deceiving messages,[23] an important element of which is the naming of the four conspirators after the holy messengers of the Koran, the bringers of the Word to a benighted people. This leads Bardolph to enquire, pertinently, about the determining role played by parents, especially in Islamic societies, in the names they choose for their children. Are we what we are called or are we called what we are? In what sense do we "become" our names? Farah, as usual, mixes his options. Though Deeriye wonders if he has unconsciously imposed his own political ideas upon his children, it is made clear that the father has taken great care not to interfere with his son's autonomy. Yet Mursal, left to go his own way, goes the way of his father. Fiona Sparrow asks, "Do we all select a different view of history and then make it repeat itself in our lives?"[24] Between the extremes of freedom and destiny, absolute self-determination and the family curse, lies the paradoxical halfway house of "voluntary determinism." By subscribing to his father's tribe-transcending nationalism, Mursal models himself on Deeriye, as Deeriye patterns his own life on, and mythicizes himself as, the Sayyid. There is no suggestion of prenatal destinies or an ancestral heritage determining human life from one generation to the next.

Perhaps the most problematic feature of *Close Sesame*, however, is its treatment of the relations between religion and politics, most particularly in its questioning of the extent to which Islam can be used to legitimize modes of government and systems of power, whatever their political colouring. "There is no one Kingdom of Islam," Farah has said, assenting to an interviewer's remark that there are "many varieties of Islamic culture, ranging from mysticism to more practical approaches to everyday life."[25] But in popular thought contemporary Islam tends to polarize into these two broad categories of "mystical" and "practical," which correspond to divisions in the Koran itself. In the first, "mystical" category fall the early verses written in Mecca, in which the Prophet is in pure spiritual communion with Allah, the central reality of the new religion, and is preoccupied by universal devotional commitments. In the second, "practical" category come the post-Hijra proselytizing verses in which the personality of the founder becomes more important: these chapters address questions of public law and the state, and presume to legislate in matters of war and the economy, marriage and divorce, inheritance and the status of women. In the latter verses the divisions of spiritual and temporal, church and state, are collapsed, and Islam is envisaged as a total way of life which excludes nothing, encompassing and codifying man's political affairs and his worldly aspirations and weaknesses along with his spiritual life. One of the extreme products of these doctrinal trends has been the modern theocratic, evangelical Islamic state, as epitomized by Iran; and Farah, along with other Muslim writers, has had his say about the militant religious leaders of these states and their arrogation of God's punitive powers in the world. Such behaviour he has pronounced "profoundly unIslamic" and in this respect his position is in line with recent reformist Islamic thinkers who have sought to depoliticize Islam and restore it to its proper spiritual and theological roots.[26] For the reformists these roots, and the essence of Islam, are to be found in the pure spirituality of its "Five Pillars": faith, prayer, alms-giving, fasting and pilgrimage. Deeriye, with the ghostly aid of Nadiifa, materially revamps these as "honour, good memory and faith in life, trust in love and friendship" (p. 26), but the primary emphasis of his beliefs remains resolutely spiritual - a phenomenon which is, surprisingly, not inconsistent with his Sayyidism. The Sayyid was, notoriously, accused by his enemies and rival poets of tyrannically exploiting Islam for political ends, even to the extent of equating the political neutrality of fellow Muslims with apostasy;[27] certainly, there is little doubt that his political retribution was ruthless, his application of Islamic law rigorous. Nevertheless, the Sayyid's primary purpose, as historians have insisted, was the straightening of the Islamic faith's path of devotion and, though this was later overshadowed by his call to national unity and his movement was bogged down in military and organizational needs, he never lost sight of this ultimate goal, as his religious poems and theological works testify.[28] Though he is remembered today as a nationalist hero, he was essentially a religious leader who became embroiled in and encumbered by political problems that distracted him from his real mission. Accordingly, Deeriye, who is himself characterised as saintly by his friends, presents the Sayyid in his sanctified role as sheikh, prophet and religious thinker as well as in his more familiar guise of warrior-hero.

How reliable and representative is Deeriye's predominantly *a*political slant on Islam, and to what extent does his religious and philosophical vision - a vision not shared by the younger characters - become the vision of the book as a whole? In the light of the pressing political circumstances of the historical situation, the weight of the book's argument would appear to lie with the conspirators, whose ideology is coherently grounded in Koranic political doctrines as formulated in the Constitution of Medina. Mursal, who wrote his doctorate on the political relevance of the Koran in an Islamic state, invokes the names of Muslim radicals who in history used the *lex talionis* to destabilize reactionary regimes by encouraging victims of political oppression to revenge themselves on the body politic itself in the form of the Head of State. In Mursal's ideal Islamic state, as in the Sayyid's, the *lex talionis* forms the cornerstone of a code that incorporates private into public justice by obviating the need for families to take their own revenge on wrongdoers. The General's so-called Islamic state is, of course, a monstrous perversion of the Koran's moral and religious teachings and political pronouncements. The dictator contravenes the Koranic code of trust and friendship by setting neighbour against neighbour and exempts his own kinsmen from the rules of retaliatory justice. He denies the Holy Book to political prisoners and, deifying himself, forces his followers to chant his own "ninety-nine names." The meanings of the Suras are twisted by satanic juvenile lapidators nurtured in the service of his regime. Accordingly, the conspirators see their task as the restoration of the errant Islamic state to its proper, ordained political course.

But if the Koran does not legitimize totalitarian dictatorship, neither does it successfully empower its revolutionary overthrow. Though its doctrines provide the ideological and inspirational fuel for an active challenge to the regime, its religious idealism and other-worldliness incapacitate the challengers on the level of practical politics, where they are no match for the astute *realpolitik* of the General. Farah mischievously gives his four conspirators the names of the Koranic messengers and indulges Deeriye's fascination with their sacred and sacrificial significances to the exclusion of their bearers' political achievements: Mursal is "the Messenger" and bringer of inspired books; Mahad is "the divine message" and "mad as a saint"; Mukhtaar is "the chosen one" and "the epitome of self-sacrifice"; Jibriil is "the mysterious angel conveying the Sacred Word" to the Prophet (pp. 71, 165). Significantly, when Samawade seeks to avenge his grandfather's injury by hurling a copy of the Koran and a cassette of the Sayyid's poetry at his assailant, Deeriye steps in to prevent the sacrilege. The utilization of either text, written or oral, as a weapon is deemed to be inconsistent with its intrinsic character and purpose, and the real nature and extent of their power is subsequently laid open to question.

The novel's politico-religious doubts and dilemmas are crystallised in the scene of Deeriye's death - an event which, characteristically, exists in two reported versions and is given no detailed investigation of motive. Though committed to non-violent opposition, Deeriye embraces Mursal's retaliatory code in order to avenge his death, partly perhaps out of the added desires to be an active participant in history as distinct from one of its legends and to offer belated recompense for the younger lives sacrificed in the struggle; and partly to demonstrate beyond all doubt, by his personal involvement, the nationalist, cross-tribal basis of the three assassination attempts. But there also appears to be present in the mind of the exhausted hero a yearning to rejoin, through death, his beloved wife, who in her final visitation is envisaged as an *houri* beckoning him to the paradisal gardens. The ambiguity which Farah's symbolism imparts to the crucial moment of martyrdom makes Deeriye's death as impenetrably aporetic as his illness; the antinomies of arrival and departure, negative presence and positive absence, are once again in evidence, with the result that the religious and political meanings tend to cancel one another out. In one of the two versions of the event, Deeriye entangles his revolver in his prayer-beads which entwine themselves around the muzzle in droll parody of the rosary and Sura attached to the tip of the Islamic warrior's lance (Deeriye's Sura is in his pocket). In this case the rosary intervenes, divinely, not to steel the heart against the infidel but to prevent Deeriye from committing an act of cold-blooded murder that would violate the basic tenets of his religious beliefs and cause him to forfeit his place in paradise. Meanwhile, at the level of practical action and political realism, the sacred object does not energize or empower the weapon but impedes it. Deeriye is at once encumbered and excused by his religious fervour, the aim of which is both the overthrow of the government and sacrificial martyrdom, redress in this world and bliss in the next. In the other version, Deeriye pulls out his rosary not as well as but *instead of* his weapon. What the symbolism offers here, however, is not so much an alternative reading of the event as a thread of the same thought. Deeriye shoots the General down not with gun-fire but with the holy purifying fire of Islam, the idealistic religious ardour which places ideals of brotherhood and friendship above clan loyalties. This dream-vision simultaneously inspires and inhibits action: it is a source of strength and solace during the long sleep of imprisonment, but has no concrete power in the waking world and issues in no constructive or effective action. Deeriye's religious vision is the equivalent of W.B.Yeats's in his poem "Byzantium," a burning intensity which yet has no external, empirical force - "the agony of flame that cannot singe a sleeve."[29] If his beloved Sayyid is a religious leader diverted by politics, Deeriye himself is, at the pragmatic level, a would-be political activist distracted and disabled by religion. At the end the reader is left wondering whether Islam is of any more practical value in the struggle against tyranny, and any more compatible with political success, than oral legend, the Sayyid's poems and all the other ideas from the past featured in the novel.

Farah's answer may be that the true and most positive values of Islam are not practical and political values but ethical and spiritual ones. At the end of this most complex and recondite work, the declared favourite of his novels,[30] these are the values that appear to have survived. As the book closes both Deeriye and his son die futile deaths but not before a number of positive strengths in traditional Somali culture have been celebrated. Prominent among these is the compelling if somewhat eroded heritage of anti-colonial struggle that makes Deeriye a charismatic figure in Somali society and a traditional rallying point and source of opposition to tyranny for all Somalis, regardless of kin and clan. Of at least equal importance, however, and reinforcing Deeriye's nationalist idealism, is the Islamic ethic of brotherhood and neighbourliness which, as instanced in the ideological alliance of Mursal and Mukhtaar, cuts across tribal divisions, proving even to Deeriye's surprise that the ties of friendship can be stronger than those of blood and demonstrating that the power of a regime that rules through division is not absolute and unchallengable. "A neighbour, according to Islamic thought, is one's closest and therefore first protector. God is our neighbour," says Deeriye, and proceeds to fulminate against his unIslamic "unneighbourly neighbours" in the house of Cigaal (p. 57). Also of importance for the vision of the trilogy as a whole is the positing, through Deeriye's behaviour in the family and at the Council of Chiefs, of an alternative, non-authoritarian model for both the domestic and national households, a counter-force to the absolute despotism of the General. Parents, in their dispensation of domestic power, pose the most significant threat to the totalitarian power of the state because it depends upon them to validate its authority. None of these opposing forces, no more than the questing integrity of young manhood in the first book and the vitality of Somali womanhood in the second, are sufficient to issue the "open sesame" to the closed door of African dictatorship, and they now seem, in retrospect, to be overridden by the dark and menacing aspects of Farah's picture of early 1980s, post-Emergency Somalia in the book. Specifically, the General's wholesale destruction of the country's cohesive political institutions through the manipulation of clan animosities and the resulting atomization into local-led factions now sound chillingly prophetic of the coming anarchy. Nevertheless, Farah, in his valediction to African dictatorship, wants the ethical imperatives of Islam, along with his alternative models of parenthood, to be noticed and viewed as possible sources of hope for the future before he moves on to the Ogaden of the next novel.

CHAPTER SEVEN
Guardians and Wards: *Maps*

Farah's sixth novel *Maps*, set in the 1977 Ogaden War, is a milestone in his fiction, marking a strange and exciting new departure. It is, however, the most formidably dense, complex and difficult of his novels and it has given not a little trouble to the few commentators who have had the temerity to tackle it. For Hilarie Kelly the book's narrator is "exasperatingly self-absorbed" and plagued by "political and sexual confusion," its style undisciplined, its conversational exchanges affectedly artificial.[1] Angela Smith regrets that the history mythologized in the novel is not part of the popular reading consciousness since most of Farah's anglophone audience will scarcely have heard of the Ogaden.[2] Jacqueline Bardolph sees the book as "une exploration, une interrogation, a plusieurs lectures possibles,"[3] and Rhonda Cobham, in similar vein, concludes that "Farah's text offers no answers" and provides no "single version of the African reality as 'true.'" The novelist, she claims, "is unremitting in his insistence that there can be no easy certainties or identities in the Somali situation or about the historical events that have produced it."[4] *Maps* is a bafflingly multidimensional work, impossible to exhaust in a single chapter, and this is reflected in a tendency among critics to focus only on selected elements of the novel: for example, the protagonist's sexual psychology (Kelly); the allegory of national identity (Bardolph); the narrative technique and the relations of politics and gender (Cobham). Although its central character is an orphan, Farah's subject is still the family; only here it is an adoptive family of guardians and wards and there is a switch from human progeny to the parenting of the nation, for Farah has woven into his human story a subtle parable about the relationship between national and ethnic identity.

In this latter aspect, *Maps* is, above all, a novel for the modern world and a text for the 1990s. In 1990 Salman Rushdie wrote in defence of his own novel: "*The Satanic Verses* celebrates hybridity, impurity, intermingling, the transformation that comes of new and unexpected combinations of human beings, cultures, ideas, politics, movies, songs. It rejoices in mongrelization and fears the absolutism of the Pure. *Melange*, hotchpotch, a bit of this and a bit of that is *how newness enters the world*. It is the great possibility that mass migration gives the world."[5] Barely were these words in print when the break-up of Central and Eastern Europe in the wake of the collapse of the Soviet Union began to release resurgent micronationalisms which immediately reversed this process. Perhaps the most startling and unforeseen consequence of the disintegration of the Soviet empire has been a reversion to absolutist ideas of the "ethnic nation" - ideas that have habitually inclined towards uncharitable views of the "migrant" or "minority" stranger and to the opinion that, in Rushdie's words, "intermingling with a different culture will inevitably weaken and ruin their own." On the African continent, where narrow tribal nationalisms have long overridden the constructs of political geography, a nomadic fiction like Farah's, drawing upon many sources and readings in many of the world's literatures, is itself a living testament to the process of cultural mongrelization of which Rushdie speaks and is a ready weapon against ethnic exclusiveness. *Maps* dramatizes, in threnodic form, the resistance to this process of universal hybridization by resurrected ethnocentrisms.

Maps is the story of Askar, an orphaned Somali child of the disputed Ogaden, and his shifting relationship with his adoptive mother Misra, an Oromo woman from the Ethiopian Highlands who is doubtfully accused of betraying the Somali army to the forces of her homeland during Ethiopia's reconquest of the Ogaden and is murdered by the Western Somali Liberation Front, of which Askar is a member. Indeed, on the last page of the novel Askar is arrested by the Mogadiscio police, presumably on suspicion of having had a hand in her murder. Askar's retrospective narrative, which is told in turns in the first, third, and speculative second person ("You are a question to yourself [...]. You doubt, at times, if you exist outside your own thoughts"),[6] recounts the traumas and triumphs of his Ogadenese childhood spent with Misra and, more briefly, his adolescence in Mogadiscio with an adoptive uncle and aunt. The narrative is haunted throughout by memories and intuitions of his foster mother's physical presence and of a sometimes excruciating intimacy with her, dating from the crucial early years. This bodily closeness, which allows the motherless male child and the childless surrogate mother to live, complementarily, inside each other, later resists the abstract intellectual hatreds of creed and country that are awakened by the Somali-Ethiopian War in the Ogaden.

Maps explores the problematics of ethnicity and, accordingly, features a number of fables of national identity, not all of which are reliable. Most suspect are those which entail feminine genderings of the independent nation, drawing up categoric parallels and oppositions along politico-sexual lines. In one such fable unfolded by a Somali poet, Somalia, portrayed as a beautiful woman, freely accepts the advances of five suitors. In the allegoric scheme, these represent the original five territories of Greater Somalia, and she conceives children by each of them, three of which miscarry: namely, French Djibouti, Kenya's Northeastern province, and the Ogaden region of Ethiopia, each of which continues to lie outside the Somali Republic constituted at independence from the former British and Italian Somalilands. The figure in the novel whose personal history approximates closest to the archetype in the fable is in fact Misra, who, ironically, is not a native Somali though she has done more than enough to earn Somali status: she fosters a Somali child and teaches it its national language and folklore; works in slave conditions in a Somali-Ogaden household where she is sexually abused by Somali men; and is, at last, doubtfully accused of treachery by them in the Ogaden war and murdered. When the fable is translated into the actualities of Misra's life story, the correspondences become apparent. She too is pursued by five men, some of them originating from the disputed homeland territories; only in her case she is the object of their largely unwanted sexual attentions. These are the Amhara warrior who abducts her from the Ethiopian Highlands as a child; the Muslim Abdullah who adopts her as his daughter and then forces her to become his wife; the Qotto teacher Aw-Adan who uses her sexually and finally betrays her to the Western Somali Liberation Front; Askar's despised Ogadenese uncle, Qorrax; and the Ethiopian captain with whom she forms a liaison in the Ogaden war. In Misra's story the miscarriages in the national fable become the abortions forced upon her by Qorrax and Aw-Adan. In each of these relationships except the last (even then, we are told of the cruelty of the Ethiopian captain), Misra, as the woman Somalia, is the abused, enslaved victim of brutal patriarchal tyranny, and Farah's point is clearly that this is the most fitting form for the image to take in the modern context. If Misra fails as an image of a free Somalia or a free Somali Ogaden, it is not because she is a foreigner of mixed Oromo and Amhara descent, but because no woman in the Horn of Africa can serve in a signifying system which indulges in the cliched gendering of national freedom in falsely heroic and idealized terms. A more appropriately negative metaphor of Woman as Nation in this part of the continent is the Camel, the "Mother of Men" who, in Askar's childhood anecdote, is held captive and blindfolded and, when untethered and freed from foreign masters by her men, can only die because when they remove her blindfold they neglect to provide her with any enlightened vision and hope for the future.[7] Independence and the reunification of its territories cannot make a nation free if half of its population are still slaves; if women still depend for their identities upon men and, as in Misra's case, cannot even establish their citizenship without oaths sworn by a couple of male witnesses. In the fable of the woman and her five suitors it is, moreover, significant that, although the political tenor of the metaphor connotes an expansive, unifying generosity, it is partly eclipsed by its sexual vehicle, which presents the woman as promiscuous, as a treacherous whore. This overshadowing is, in fact, more faithfully revealing of continuing patriarchal attitudes and prevailing Somali male psychology. The Somali poets, Misra tells Askar, see their country "as a woman [...] who has made it her habit to betray her man" (p. 98), and the comments of Askar's schoolmates seem to uphold the stereotype: "Why, if she isn't your mother, your sister or your wife, a woman is a whore" (p. 52). The nation is disingenuously gendered as an imaginary woman, for whom lives must be laid down, by patriots who in fact despise the real women in their daily lives.

The attempt to endow gender with national political significance in the Somali context finds its *reductio ad absurdam* in the novel's eccentric telescoping of national and biological fates. In *Maps* there is a deliberately puzzling indeterminacy about where metaphor ends and reality starts, and a habitual erosion of the public into the personal, and of topographical into physiological space, which allows Askar to view the political destiny and military fortunes of the nation, analogically, through his adoptive mother's biological rhythms. Specifically, after Misra's vengeful pack-rape by WSLF patriots, he sees the deaths of a hundred Somali soldiers whom she is accused of betraying in terms of the death-cycle of her own body. Askar's charts are simultaneously military and menstrual maps, historical and contraceptive calendars on which the green-clad Somali troops who march backwards and forwards across the Ogaden correspond, with a perverse ingenuity, to the green-ringed dates for safe (in the sense of non-procreative) sex. In such instances the reader is put in mind of remarks like John S. Mbiti's, in *African Religions and Philosophy*[8], about the African woman's equation of infertility with genocide, construing the failure to conceive as a kind of killing, the murder of not creating, or, in Askar's words, "the cycle of life and death, the circle ending where it began - the flow of menstruation, of death ascertained" (p. 31). In Askar's lurid fantasy, which fetishizes menstruation into something over and above its simple biological function, this idea is realized with a graphic vengeance:

> Was it true that she had betrayed a trust and set a trap in which a hundred Kallafo warriors lost their lives? [...] He then remembered that living with Misra wasn't always full of exhilaration and happiness, that there were moments of sadness, that it wasn't always fun. It had its pains, its agonies, its ups and downs, especially when the cavity of her womb overflowed with a tautology flow of blood once every month. When this occurred, she was fierce to look at, she was ugly, her hair uncombed, her spirit low, and she was short-tempered, beating him often, losing her temper with him. She was depressive, suicidal, no, homicidal. (p. 48)

In this instance the metaphoric vehicle seems to have slipped its tenor and become a reality in its own right, recasting the political haemorrhagings of the nation as massacres of the menses; as atrocities inflicted, implausibly, by a vengeful premenstrual terrorism wielded over the lives of men. The fantastic distortions of Askar's paranoid male psychology literally invest the woman's menstrual trauma with homicidal propensities. Misra's breast cancer is similarly endowed with "evil" elements over and above the mere physiological phenomenon, with the result that she comes to be regarded as an extension of her disease, as malignant as her tumour. In Askar's narrative speculations the tumour acquires the ancient punitive associations of the "canker of guilt," something which she has both caused and deserved, and which her body, by its own inner logic, has brought upon itself. Moreover, cancer cells, in the mythology of the disease as described by Susan Sontag,[9] are often said to "spread," "proliferate" and "invade"; the patient's body becomes a besieged citadel infiltrated by enemy cells that represent the non-self. Cancer, says Sontag, is therefore "the disease of the Other," and Askar, despite his physical closeness to Misra, uses the disease hysterically to "other" her into the alien menace, the enemy whose blood is to be vengefully drunk, her heart torn out and her flesh devoured (pp. 213-14, 221).

There are in Farah's novel more reliable indices to the relations between a nation and its members than a courtesan and her lovers, a she-camel and its male liberators, a woman's menstrual cycle and the pathology of breast cancer. One less limited and more reliable system of signification - not surprisingly in Farah's fiction, where domestic and political patriarchies are mutually reinforcing - is to be found in the roles of parents, or guardians, and children. In *Maps* the post-colonial nation is not so much "gendered" as "engendered," in the sense of parented - or, more precisely in this case, foster-parented.

Nationality categories are, arguably, most accurately read through the positions assumed by the novel's various surrogate parents towards their charges. Conversely, the destabilization of these categories is best perceived through a series of pseudo-incestuous role-reversals which subvert these positions by breaking down customary differentials (parent and child, adult and infant, patriarch and ward). To this primary tropology the specifics of gender *per se* are secondary in importance.

The postcolonial territory of Askar's birth is, like Askar himself, without natural parentage. Neither is it self-creating, as Askar fancies himself to be - "I had made myself, as though I was my own creation" (p. 23) - though it may have the opportunity to take charge of its own destiny. Such territories are, in reality, the imaginative constructs of colonial and postcolonial cartographers (British, Italian, Ethiopian, Somali), conceived not biologically but intellectually: Askar, the human analogue of the Somali Ogaden, describes himself as "a creature given birth to by notions formulated in heads, a creature brought into being by ideas" (p. 3). Such creatures are not bonded together organically in the way that families are but are adopted beings with adopted identities defined by adoptive parents, and Farah sustains the analogies between the child's ties with the family and the individual's more artificial ties with the nation only by replacing Askar's real parents with a range of surrogates and guardians. Misra, who nominally represents the Ethiopian occupier but whose Oromo culture has deep ties with the Somali one, is in fact only one of Askar-Ogaden's many guardians. There are also the childless urban intellectuals Hilaal and Salaado, who represent the modern Somali Republic, seeking to complete itself by the addition of the motherless child of the Ogaden; the Koranic schoolteacher Aw-Adan, who represents the unifying power of Islam; and the brutal Ogadenese-Somali Uncle Qorrax, who can impart only suffering to his charges. At the end of the book each of Askar-Ogaden's five guardians have had parts of themselves chopped away. Misra undergoes a mastectomy (and is then murdered and mutilated, her heart torn out); Hilaal has had a vasectomy, his wife Salaado a hysterectomy; Aw-Adan has had a leg amputated; and Qorrax has had blood exacted. These truncations seem to signify, allegorically, both the dismemberment of the Ogaden and the further fragmentation of Greater Somalia into its five territories.

In the book's parabolic scheme Askar, representing the Ogaden, is born to two patriotic martyrs who give their lives for the cause of its liberation from Ethiopian occupation: his father dies on the day of his birth and his mother soon afterwards. He is thus the posthumous mythic offspring of Somali nationalist aspiration and the motherland of the Republic (though the purity of the mother's ethnic origins are not inquired into too closely), and he signifies what is salvaged by his country from the colonial carve-up of the Horn of Africa (his mother's unread journal, predating Somali orthography, is written in Italian). Askar-Ogaden is then, strangely, entrusted by her to the "enemy" in the form of the Oromo-Amhara woman Misra, who is not of the same blood as the child, whether in the matrilineal or ethnic senses. The child's budding nationalist aspirations are subsequently grounded in the special stifling, suffocating intimacy generated by the one-parent-one-child family situation, in which the gender-confused male child first identifies with and then seeks to exorcize the oppressively close maternal presence. As he grows up Askar feels a natural need to live a life independent of Misra and expresses the desire of each man to kill the "mother" in him: "To live, I will have to kill you" (p. 57). But these emotions get mixed up with a felt imperative to shoulder the burden of his biological inheritance, left him by his natural mother, by defending his country from the people of his nurturing mother, even though he has only the most theoretical sense of the former, compared with the intensely felt proximity of the latter (as we shall see later, Askar's strange obsession with "a woman living inside him" relates to his dead biological mother, not his living adoptive one).

At his circumcision, which is his first lesson in frontiers, Askar is ritually separated from Misra and begins to define his "specific" Somali adult maleness against his "generic" Ethiopian mother-figure (the terms are those of his uncle Hilaal, who argues that Somalis have their own unique and exclusive language, culture and destiny, while "Ethiopia" is a "generic notion, expansive, inclusive," being merely "the generic name of an unclassified mass of different peoples"; p. 148). After this painful separation he is given his first maps and calendars and these become the "mental charts" on which he measures, in time and space, both "the uncoverable distance between Misra and himself" (p. 97) and the Somali advances and retreats in the Ogaden. Significantly, as the war in the Ogaden escalates, the seven-year-old Askar is physically removed to Mogadiscio and his childhood dependence on Misra comes to an end. Askar's first steps towards psychological independence have thus initiated, quite fortuitously, an involvement with his homeland's political independence, and from the moment of his arrival in the Somali capital, national military progress in the Ogaden is measured, symbolically, by the distance that has grown between the Somali child and the adoptive "Ethiopian" mother whose foreign presence within him he feels he must rid himself of. This physical distance between "your anatomy and mine" (p. 18) becomes, increasingly, a perceptual distance between her physical reality and his mental image of her. When he meets her again in the capital years later, he feels "totally detached" and "weaned" from his "mother-figure," for "in the process of looking for a substitute, he had found another - Somalia, his mother country" (p. 96). He now feels that he can espouse one of his rival adoptive mothers only by denying the other, and the earlier ominous words of his childhood, "To live, I will have to kill you," now take on, in the quite different context of her suspected betrayal of the Somali army, the tone of patriotic duty. Yet his sense of his separate identity is continually undermined by his long and deep intimacy with Misra and, when placed beside this, his claims for the primacy within himself of his unknown biological mother are less than persuasive. Indeed, Askar is culturally formed and moulded by Misra in his upbringing. For example, his fantasy that he is one of the race of epic miracle children who kill their mothers at birth is implanted in his mind by Misra's Oromo oral tales and folklore: thus, even the idea of his natural mother's special moral claim upon him derives, ironically, from the culture of his adoptive mother.

In the historical period covered by the novel Askar, like his beloved Ogaden, is separated from both his mothers - from his Somali motherland at his birth and from his Ethiopian stepmother at her death - and the latter separation, in the lives of both individual and nation, is the costlier affair. During the "tragic weekend" in which Russian-backed Ethiopian forces retake the Ogaden and a total of six hundred Somali patriots are betrayed and massacred, refugees flood into Mogadiscio, among them Misra, accused specifically of the betrayal of the hundred Kallafo men. Embarrassed by her arrival in the capital and by reports of her reputed treachery, Askar is then further traumatized by her final abduction and death at the hands of the Liberation Front (her mutilated corpse is fished out of the bay). He falls mysteriously ill at each of these crisis points and it later transpires that one of the things he may have been evading through sickness is his own ill-defined complicity with Misra's murder, for which he is apparently detained and interrogated at the end of the novel. In this respect *Maps* might be compared with Graham Swift's novel *Waterland*, in which the protagonist also tries to hide from himself (and from the reader) his involvement in a murder. The difference is that whereas Swift, a late modernist-realist, is concerned with the ultimate meaning of the deed performed by the guilty party and with the gradual revelation of his hidden traumas, Farah, in more postmodernist fashion, poses the ontological question of *what* it is that the narrator has done and is now concealing from himself, or indeed, *whether* he has done anything (which things are clear neither to the reader nor to the character himself). There are, for example, two passages in *Maps* - where Askar pictures a soldier standing over a wounded woman with a blood-stained knife and then imagines himself a fish feeding from Misra's blood (pp. 211, 214) - which could be construed to mean that Askar, if not the initiator, was at least an accomplice in Misra's murder and dismemberment. But as both of these passages are presented in the form of dream sequences, it is difficult to say exactly what is happening or when, or at what level the images are meant to be read.

To return to the fable of national identity: the association of Misra with the foreign occupation of the Ogaden is ultimately a spurious one. She is, after all, an Amharic-speaking Oromo, not a full-blooded Ethiopian, and she has more natural affinity with the occupied zone than with the occupier. She is herself an occupied possession on Somali as on Ethiopian territory, a slave-girl sexually colonized by a host of "uncles": the Ogaden's symbolic guardian is herself the guarded property, violated by various occupying patriarchal wardens. Also Misra, like Askar, is an uprooted orphan and her Oromo culture, like the Somali one, has been historically marginalized by its orality and oppressed by a literate Ethiopia. She is, in fact, doubly displaced: first as an Oromo living in Ethiopia and forced to speak the language of the dominant Amharic culture, and then as an "Ethiopian" reviled by Somali ethnocentrism. Ironically, Misra is, much more precisely than Askar, a fitting image of the Ogaden which she is accused of betraying. Like the Ogaden, she is brutally abused by Somali patriarchy, is raped by her supposed defenders (the Liberation Front patriots), and is finally, mutilated and dismembered, her heart torn out by war. For the bigoted members of the WSLF, who are convinced they need no proof of Misra's guilt, she is the diseased part of the Somali heritage, a foreign cancer to be probed and surgically removed (such is their perverse reading of her mastectomy). But those who live fragmentarily, through a number of cultures as Misra does, always have missing parts of themselves elsewhere, on the other side of some border, whether in Mogadiscio or in Ethiopia. Misra is not a unitary being who can be comprehensively enclosed and defined by maps but represents the various parts of cultures and countries - Oromo, Ethiopian, Somali - which are to be found in mongrelized, migration-prone areas like the Ogaden. Farah has said that the Kallafo of his Ogaden childhood "boasted a Somali-speaking civilian population, a large Arab community engaged in business, as well as Amharic-speaking soldiers [...] recruited from all the ethnic groupings of which the Ethiopian empire comprised."[10] Although Askar likes to think of Ethiopia as a "patchwork country," it is really the Ogaden - crossed, as the veteran soldier remarks, by different waves of migrants twenty, fifty, or a hundred years apart over a period of centuries - which best expresses the irretrievable hybridization of cultural reality. This hybridization is most keenly represented in the novel by Misra.

Misra is the daughter of an Amhara nobleman and an Oromo servant, she lives with a Somali family, and has Qotto and Ethiopian lovers. Accordingly, like the woman in the fable, she has access to and concourse with all of the fertile neighboring micro-cultures and tribal nationalisms by which the Ogaden is hedged around and diversified, in spite of its narrowly ethnocentric efforts to resist them. Creative energy, it seems, lives, liminally, along these borders: Askar notes that two-thirds of Somalia's major poets come from its marginal territories and that one such peripheral people, the Boran, provide the Mogadiscio *mingis* with its ceremonial language. Appropriately, the Ogaden is symbolically entrusted by Askar's real mother to one such border person, to one of mixed descent and therefore with a choice of identities. This entrustment by a Somali woman to an Oromo servant-girl, reaching across artificial boundaries erected by male nationalistic obsessions, is done, it seems, not vengefully, but rather in a spirit of expiation and in recognition of their common Cushitic heritage and interpenetrating cultures. The reputedly "specific" Somali culture which uncle Hilaal theorizes about at length is seen, in reality, to participate in a broader generic group and it is surely no accident that, for all his talk of Somali specificity, there are actually few "pure" Somalis in the novel and those who exist are surrounded by people of Oromo, Qotto, Boran, Adenese, Arab, and Ethiopian extraction. Misra's name exists in three of these languages and in its Somali form is an incomplete version of the Ethiopian "Misrat," meaning "foundation of the earth": thus it refers to the elemental, non-partisan character of the disputed strip of ground, which does not discriminate between its diverse occupying nationalities and the rival maps that overlay it like the layers of a palimpsest. Interestingly, in the illustrator's design on the cover of the English edition the desert earth is depicted as covering and almost obscuring the map instead of the other way round, thus catching something of the spirit of Farah's novel. The name "Misrat," indicating the unmapped, unfrontiered earth, is an appropriately loose signifier for an area as diverse as the Ogaden and is certainly more appropriate in this role than the name "Askar," whose bearer bears no more than his name - certainly, he does not bear arms, or even true witness, for his country.

Two key motifs in the novel contest this linguistic and cultural hybridization and play contrapuntally against them in the text: the first is incest, the second maps. Askar says quite early in the novel that Misra regards the fabric of Somali society as "basically incestuous" (p. 26). In the course of his narrative incest becomes an expressive image of the narrow, inward-looking ethnocentrism of Somali culture, its failure to diversify itself by recognizing its kinship with neighbouring peoples in a broader generic family. But it is also used to demonstrate the way in which the patriarchal abuse of power in the Ogaden shores up micronational divisions among its chequered subjects. The region's paternal guardians appear to make a habit of abusing the foreign wards entrusted to their care and protection, committing a figurative incest and reinstituting damaging stereotypes of nationality and race by identifying the national, ethnic or religious "other" as a mere object of denigration. The Somali boys are abused by the Adenese; the Ogaden foster-child by the disciplinarian schoolteacher and lover of his adoptive mother; and the abducted Oromo girl by the Somali patriarchs and the wealthy Muslim Abdullah who forces her to switch roles from adopted daughter to wife. The new Ethiopian guardians respond in kind to the Somalis when retaking the Ogaden. In each case the child looks to its false foster-parent, as the Ogaden to its latest political guardian, for self-definition, moral example, and leadership - only to find paternal and avuncular responsibilities betrayed and traditional relationships inverted. "Uncles" become rapists, fathers husbands, daughters wives (as we shall see later, Askar is himself not innocent of this incestuous abuse of power). The guardian disingenuously claims sole rights to his ward, as does the current custodial power to its "people" in the occupied territory, and then - since they are not, in fact, his "people" or blood-kin - assumes licence to humiliate them in crypto-incestuous fashion.

On the narrative level, Misra's relations with Askar are not entirely normal. But the Ogaden is symbolically entrusted to her because, in the Brechtian phrase, she is good for it, and its paternal guardians - be they Somali, Qotto or Amhara - clearly are not. "We're in each other's life now. No more wars. We're a family," says Hilaal as he hugs Askar to him, and in this he speaks, unconsciously, for the multicultural, mongrel spirit of the

Ogaden, which desires only that its various guardians live at peace with its occupants and they with one another. Misra is the good guardian because, unlike the novel's paternal guardians and their shifting sectarian political counterparts, she is sufficiently conversant with all her people's cultures to make allowance for their different partisan relevancies and myopias. She is the true mother who sees all the blind spots on her child's body and "soaps them all and, in the end, washes them clean" (pp. 110-11). When she admits to buying milk for the Ethiopian soldiers, she protests that "she was doing something for 'her people'," but then adds the comment, "the problem is, who are 'my people'?" (p. 184). The phrase is, of course, deliberately ambiguous. Both sides are "her people" and she provides both with what they most need: milk for the Ethiopians, money for the Somalis. Misra serves all members of her larger, generic Ogaden "family," giving to each what is good for them and overriding the incestuous inwardness of Somali ethnicity.

The second and stronger bastion of resistance to cultural and linguistic diversification is Askar's maps. Farah has said of the colonial maps of Africa that "we should redraw [them] according to our economic and psychological and social needs, and not accept the nonsensical frontiers carved out of our regions."[11] And yet it is no accident that Askar has a nostalgic hankering for the time, during World War Two, when all of the Somali territories except for Djibouti were under a single, colonial administration: his own politico-linguistic map of Greater Somalia is, in reality, as much a fiction of cultural geography as the colonial maps were figments of political geography. History, Hilaal reminds us, is made by those who have access to sign-systems (p. 168) and is imposed upon those who have not, and the coercive cartographic enclosures enforced by the newly-literate Somalis override socio-political (and, increasingly, cultural) divisions as the old Western imperial ones overrode ethnic and linguistic barriers; their ethnocentric organization of political space is, arguably, as distortive of reality as the Mercator projection's Eurocentric organization of geographical space. The Somalis of the WSLF regard their people as united by language, divided by maps, and the independent nation-state of the Somali Republic imagines that its cultural-linguistic "specificity" gives it a unique claim on those territories where Somali, in one fashion or another, is still spoken. This is, of course, shaky as a political proposition: Hausa and Yoruba speakers live in pockets all over West Africa as do Somali speakers in marginal territories spread over East Africa and the Horn, and, since "Biafra," the Ibos might make much the same nationalistic claim. But the real objection to the new cartographic hegemony is that it claims to unite people who, both linguistically and in other respects, are becoming more and more diverse - who have in fact become irredeemably mongrelized - while it artificially sets apart other groups of people who, in reality, are much more closely bonded. In the former category are the Somalis scattered through Kenya and Tanzania, like the tutor of Cusmaan, Askar's intellectual mentor in Mogadiscio. These, when they are not speaking Swahili, use a bastardized, ungrammatical form of Somali similar to that spoken by the Ogadenese Somalis, and their subscription to Somali cultural values is as adulterated and compromised by the dominant host-cultures as is that of the Ogadenese marginal groups, the Oromo and Qotto, by the Somali one. Much closer to home, the Westernized urbanites of Mogadiscio, at the hub of the nation-state, do not identify closely with their Ogadenese brethren but snobbishly regard them not only as linguistically incompetent but also as lacking in self-sufficiency and wholeness. No sooner has Hilaal declared categorically that "you are either a Somali or you aren't" (p. 148) than he proceeds to postulate a halfway classification of extraterritorial "unpersons" who cannot be admitted to a full Somali identity. All the indicators suggest that the linguistic homogeneity and cultural exclusiveness of Greater Somalia are rapidly disintegrating. Conversely, in the second category there is Misra, a non-ethnic Somali speaker who, though fully acculturated, is automatically mistrusted and is denied a place on her Somali ward's identity papers - a place which she has surely earned by fostering and educating him and suffering abuse in his Somali-Ogaden household. Meanwhile, in the same Greater Somalia where children are made to learn their genealogies by heart as proof of ethnicity,[12] honorary citizenship is granted to another non-ethnic Somali, the sullen Qotto schoolteacher Aw-Adan, for no other reason than that his Arabic input into Somali culture is, politically, more acceptable than her Amharic one (significantly it is Aw-Adan, whose loyalty is never questioned, who accuses Misra of treachery, thus, perhaps, making his own insecure position a little safer by denouncing another foreigner).

What is a Somali and what does it mean to be one? The question opens up a Pandora's box of political, ethnic and moral quandaries. Is it to speak or to read the language, or to be born in the homeland or in one of its territories? (In fact, as we have already noticed, few of the novel's Somali speakers are Somalis by birth). Is it to be a patriot in the cause of the Ogaden? - in which case what right has Qorrax, who openly collaborates with the Ethiopian conquerors, to his Somali identity? Who, if anyone, is fit to be political guardian of the disputed Ogaden territory to which Somalia lays claim? Who can claim to have "authored" it parentally? The criteria for nationhood, like the Somali map of the Ogaden which ignores its multilingual character and fifty per cent Amharic-speaking population, are increasingly erratic and capricious, leaving little ground for belief in anything that could be described as a "pure" or "authentic" Somali identity. In one way or another, each of the novel's characters stands, like the girl in Askar's dream, "in a borrowed skin" and the Somali map, with its peculiarly monolithic contours and fine disregard of multiculuralism, provides an inexact, inadequate model of reality.

Nationality and gender are equally elusive of definition in this work, a country being as hard to describe as a mother's sphere of influence over a male child. Not surprisingly, therefore, the strongest component in the cultural spillover from nationality categories into surrounding "enemy" territory is the relationship of Misra and Askar. Farah's remark about his novels that "an intellectual and psychological debate is going on between two selves - the woman's self in the man, the man's self in the woman,"[13] is especially relevant to *Maps*, the role-interchanges by Hilaal and Salaado being only the most overt of the androgynous fusions that cut across the novel's polarised political landscapes. The motherless boy and childless mother are complementary opposites who, as a result of close physical intimacy during Askar's infancy, are able to reach across national borderlines to live inside each other (like the trans-sexual spirits of the *mingis* ceremony), accounting for that part of the other being which is least aware and least in possession of itself. "Body is truth," says Hilaal, and Farah, in *Maps*, has arguably written the first African novel of the body, with a great mass of body-literature ranged behind it (to the acknowledged sources - Freud, Wilhelm Reich, Otto Rank - could be added the body-poetesses Sylvia Plath and Anne Sexton, the body-novelists Gunter Grass and D.M.Thomas). The body seems in the novel to be an alternative way of constituting identity, more reliable than maps. Askar knows his adoptive mother wholly through the body, which operates according to its own instinctive wisdom and logic, making "autonomous decisions" (p. 221) which override political hatreds. His failure lies in his inability to trust to this special knowledge, this excruciating intimacy that makes him think he can taste the blood of Misra's death in his mouth. His unpardonable sin is his psychological surrender of Misra's reality to the female stereotype of the betrayer, to what Hilaal sees as the scapegoat for the misfortunes that men bring upon their own heads. Misra is approachable only through intuitions aroused by her physical presence - to feel her "truth" Askar must "touch her in a dark room" - and Askar opposes to this tactual presence the nationality-ridden world of maps, denoting the distancing and deathly mental control of reality through the imposition of boundaries.

Maps, like the wars fought over them to redraw national terrains, distort and destroy ("wars are rivers that burn," says Hilaal); and from the initial presentation of them to the child by Qorrax, dressed in mourning and prophesying a fatality, to the massacre of the six hundred in the Ogaden, they are attended by funereal images. Askar, in his new persona of fledgling Somali partisan, claims that his maps "invent nothing": rather, they "copy a given reality" (p. 216). Yet the "notional truths" expressed by the Somali maps correspond to the political actuality of the Horn of Africa as little as Askar's moral conception of Misra (who has no undestanding of maps) coincides with the real woman. "Misra was before him again," he imagines their reunion in Mogadiscio, "there she was, real as the border" (p. 127) - or as *un*real, since the two are equally figmentary. Misra, like the political map of the territory of which she is the figurative custodian, is in his consciousness a floating signifier, zoned into many stereotyped figures and rival fantasy embodiments: on one side, mother-martyr and victimized nation; on the other, wicked stepmother, betrayer, and national enemy (since Askar-Ogaden is a contested possession, she is bound to be a betrayer in someone's eyes). A nominal sense of reality so prevails over the actual that at one point Askar even thinks of her as "a creature of his own invention" (p. 107). Thus it is difficult to say exactly what does constitute her reality, since she seems (like the Ogaden) to exist solely through the guardians and wards who, from her nobleman father and adoptive father-turned-husband to Askar and her Ethiopian lover, control her existence in one way or another.

Askar, the girl in the dream tells him, is "almost always satisfied with the surface of things [...] a mirror in which your features [...] may be reflected" (p. 130). For him, Misra is a perfect image of the Ogaden insofar as both are mirrors in which the beholder sees his own desires reflected, and maps, like mirrors, reflect the dispositions of their makers. "There is truth in maps," Hilaal concedes, but adds the rider: "The question is, does truth change? [...] The Ogaden, as Somali, is truth. To the Ethiopian map-maker, the Ogaden, as Somali, is untruth" (pp. 217-18). The "truth" of maps is a highly subjective, ethnocentric kind of truth, and the stable identity presupposed by the idealistic vision of the map-maker non-existent.

Inevitably, since Askar is one of the map-makers and Misra is, symbolically, part of the shifting, hybridized reality which is mapped, the nationality categories unsettled by Askar's extreme cartographic relativism come to have some bearing upon the novel's equally unstable gender categories. Significantly, the trans-sexual spirits of the *mingis* are also instruments for the interpenetration of national and marginal cultures, bringing the Boran language into the Somali heartland, and it is no accident that Farah uses gender confusion to demonstrate that even Somalia's much-vaunted linguistic homogeneity is not unassailable. The peculiar misgenderings of the language once found only in "non-native" peripheral territories subject to foreign influence (p. 161) are now brought back to the urban centre by refugees from the Ogaden and elsewhere, and these all contribute importantly to the broader, interpenetrative matrix of cultural forces which have come to constitute Somali identity. The misgendering of language, however, is less problematic than the misgendering of people; and because the categories of nation and gender in the book appear to be neither wholly independent nor vitally interdependent, it is never certain how far one can be used as an index for the other. Askar's nationalistic aspirations, as we have seen, are grounded problematically in the oppressive intimacy of the one-parent family and in the subsequent attempt to liberate his "male" identity from the acute maternal presence. These "male" and "female" identities later acquire political meaning in the allegoric scheme as, respectively, "Somali" and "Ethiopian," but the nationalistic dimension has the air of something added in retrospect, as an afterthought. It is, after all, a historical accident that, after the loss of the Ogaden, the mother figure and the Ethiopian "enemy" become, arbitrarily, one and the same person, making the surrogate parent a "false mother" in an additional sense. Askar's misogynistic rejection of Misra when she takes an Ethiopian lover then merely receives external reinforcement from his xenophobic Somali ethnocentrism; that her lover is an "enemy" Ethiopian is politically convenient for his newfound patriotism. In fact, the primary poles of the conflict raging within him, which causes him, alternately, to villify and vindicate his stepmother, are not personal loyalty and nationalistic hatred but, beneath the camouflage these provide, guilt and the childhood sexual jealousies which are revived by this liaison.

The Somali psychologist Hussein A.Bulham has said in his review of the novel that "Askar's personal crises are more intellectual than affective, more contrived than lived."[14] Indeed, there is a curiously willed, deliberate quality, and at times an abstract, fantastical element, in Askar's behaviour, particularly in his obsessive adherence to the idea that there is a "woman living inside" him and his near-fetishistic treatment of menstruation. These, in fact, have curiously little to do directly, and in a cross-genderly way, with Misra, the woman who is most physically present in his life. They seem rather to be tied up with a theoretical guilt complex over his biological mother, "she who claimed she 'lived' in him who had survived her" (p. 105), and whom he accuses himself of killing at his own birth: "I feel as if my mother's death was my birth, or, if you prefer, her death gave birth to me" (p. 151). Guilt is the means by which he wills his biological mother to survive in himself and it is after brooding not over Misra but over this spectral figure that he imagines himself to have menstruated. The feeling is thus more filial than sexual, having to do with his literal "engenderer" rather than with gender as such: it is specifically the mother rather than the woman in him, and the native, not the foreigner, whom Askar desires by turns to preserve or to kill. At the psycho-level of the narrative the trans-gendering interchanges of stepmother and son can, in the last analysis, be dismissed as the neurotic fantasies of an alternately mother-fixated and misogynistically self-centred child; and at the level of realism, they can be seen to reaffirm rather than erode sexual categories.

It is possible, of course, to argue that this reductive element in Askar's behaviour responds only to a conventional psychological-realist reading of the text and that such readings need to take into account more expansive postmodernist currents which also feature in the construction of his character. Askar appears to straddle not only sexual and national but also ontological boundaries. He aspires to be, at once, "half-man, half-child," male and female, ethnocentric Somali and culturally diverse Ogadenese. He also fancies himself to be both a real child and an epic miracle child who was present at his own birth (one who has "met death when not quite a being") and who is able to argue metaphysics at the age of seven. He claims to hold "simultaneously multiple citizenships of different kingdoms: that of the living and that of the dead; not to mention that of being an infant and an adult at the same time" (p. 11). Like his prototypes, Grass's Oskar and Rushdie's Saleem, he is a self-professedly liminal creature, an occupant of the between-worlds space of the zone, that improbable area in postmodernist fiction where these incongruous elements can coexist. Like them, he appears at times to be a composite imaginative construct put together from diverse sources and finally, as he struggles on the last page of the novel to free himself of blame for Misra's death, fragmenting back into its constituent parts: defendant, plaintiff, juror, witness, judge and audience. It is also arguable that the novel attaches considerable value to the idea of an indeterminate area of experience, a liminal third space (Askar is Misra's "third breast" and "third leg") which exists between alternatives; that it opens out creatively into new imaginative regions, new areas of possibility which transcend the binary polarities of male and female, child and adult, Somali and Ethiopian. Its mode of reality may finally, therefore, be of a surreal or supra-rational nature, unboundaried and unmappable. After reading *Maps* four times, I must confess that I am still undecided whether psychological realism or postmodern experimentalism is the dominant mode of the novel.

It does seem to me, however, that at the base level of common-sense realism there are strict limits to Askar's indeterminacy and that these have not been sufficiently stressed. "Every image floats vaguely in a sea of doubt," declares one of the book's Conradian epigraphs, "and the doubt itself is lost in an unexplored universe of incertitude" (p. 133). Nevertheless, the doubts and uncertainties, the ambiguities and contradictions in Askar's consciousness have a way of resolving themselves, at the realistic level, into singular and diametric oppositions. Firstly, the fantasy that he is a miracle child is no more than that: it is quickly disposed of by Hilaal as such and, as we have seen, was apparently planted in his mind by Misra; at the level of psychological explication, his vaunted multidimensionality is the fruit of her multicultural nurturing. Secondly, even the single claim of Askar's that seems to retain any psychological validity - "of being an infant and an adult at the same time" (p. 11) - is one that to some extent overrides the novel's alleged androgynous fusions. Askar looks to Misra both as a child, for succor, and as a male adult, for submission to his patriarchal will, and it is in the latter context that his fetishistic fascination with her menstruation is best seen. Though he begins, as a child, by wanting to relieve her of some of her periodic pain - "If I had some of it, then Misra will have less of it, yes?" (p. 49) - his preoccupation eventually turns into the ultimate male fantasy of control: he imagines that he can direct, with his sanguinary stare, the one thing in the woman's life over which men have no control, thus reducing her, in his fantasy, to the ultra male-dominated object. When Askar, as a result of a urinary infection, imagines himself to have menstruated and to have felt what it is like to be a woman, he effectively collapses the options posed by Misra: "You prefer being sick to being a woman" (p. 107). In Askar's mind, to be a woman is to be periodically sick and Hilaal's remark that Misra's menstruation ceased to be excruciatingly painful after Askar's departure from the Ogaden poses a logical link between her "sickness" and his lurid imaginings (p. 228). His imaginative participation in and vicarious knowledge of Misra's traumas are, in fact, means to power and belittlement, if only in negative forms. Askar affects, hypochondriacally, a periodic sickness, becoming quasi-menstrually ill, in order to duck out of confrontations, decision-making, and the facing up to responsibility at each of the crisis-points of his life: at the betrayal of the Ogaden, Misra's subsequent arrival in Mogadiscio, and her final abduction and death at the hands of the WSLF. Menstruality is, indeed, concretely linked with the death which he fails to prevent as a result of his shirking of his responsibilities: in his dream Misra feeds the fishes with the menstrual death-flow of her own body, in the very harbour which her mutilated corpse will be fished out of (pp. 214-15). Thus, paradoxically, Askar imaginatively appropriates Misra's "female illness" in order to express sympathy and solidarity with her, but also to indulge in fantasies of power and control, and finally to dissociate himself from and abandon her. What is realized here is not so much a cross-gendering capacity to share suffering as, in a variant form, a sexual "othering" of the woman as a submissive and manipulable object, and the exercise of a male will which breaks down ego rather than gender boundaries.

Rhonda Cobham has argued that Askar's "I" voice articulates a female self which fails to recognize physical and emotional boundaries between Misra and himself.[15] It is, however, Misra who assumes "responsibility" for Askar's "body" and "thoughts" by taking the blame for his trespasses, not he who assumes an identity with her, and her very protectiveness gives him an opportunity to exercise power over her: their "common secret" is the knowledge "that I had her whole life in the power of my mouth and I could do what I wanted with it" (p. 40). Askar's solidarity with Misra is, in any case, a short-term and makeshift one, lasting only for as long as he suffers the same patriarchal brutality borne by herself. Even then, when the nocturnal male visitors force themselves upon her, the child is enraged not merely by her neglect of him but by her sexual domination by the uncles and Aw-Adan, for whom he feels an incestuous Oedipal envy. Indeed, in the early intimacies Askar passes quickly from being an infant child in androgynous interplay with its mother - "Misra who eventually tucked me into the oozy warmth between her breasts [...] so much so that I became a third breast" - to becoming a crypto-incestuous lover, lying "somewhere between her opened legs [...] as though I was a third leg" (p. 24). Cobham comments ingeniously:

> It is as if, in taking on a feminized identity through his merging with Misra, Askar becomes Misra's penis or third leg. And we can read this either as Askar's masculinization (or empowerment) of Misra, or his erasure of her as he incorporates her entire feminine identity into himself.[16]

The latter seems to me to be the likelier option and a simpler explanation to be that the "third leg" identifies Askar explicitly with the wooden leg which the crippled Aw-Adan speedily removes before intercourse with Misra and thence, vicariously, with Aw-Adan's penis:

> I remembered how fast the third leg (the wooden leg, that is) was dropped and how fast another between his legs came to raise its head, jerkily, slowly and nervously; and how the whole place drowned in the sighing endearments of Misra who called him [...] yes him of all people [...] "my man, my man, my man!" (pp. 31-32)

Misra, of course, uses the same endearments to the child Askar - "my man!" (pp. 57, 127). The child adopts a female self, and a figurative female part, only by way of asserting his real male ones. Askar participates imaginatively in Misra's sexuality only as a prelude to appropriating and incestuously exploiting it, as he "participates" in her menstruation only with a view to controlling it. Not surprisingly, the adolescent Askar is plagued by subconscious guilt over his physical attachment to his stepmother, and his elected psychological ruse for escaping this guilt is to externalize his incestuous desires and alienate them to Misra herself, thus turning the victim into the aggressor. To this end, he systematically falsifies Misra's past, accusing her of murdering her adoptive father-husband "during an excessive orgy of copulation," whereas the truth is that her guardian forced himself upon her and a likelier cause of death was the old man's sexual over-enthusiasm. The role of incestuous murderer clearly accords more closely with Askar's newly-adopted image of Misra as "enemy-barbarian." More incredibly, he recasts her Ethiopian lover, in his imagination, as a half-brother with whom she enters into a sexual liaison in full knowledge of their blood ties, thus transferring his own incestuous desires to the lover and substituting for him in his own fantasies. It is significant that Misra allows herself to be blackmailed into sleeping with uncle Qorrax because only by so doing is she able to sleep with Askar, thus innocently implicating the child in her sexual humiliation and linking him with Qorrax's parallel quasi-incest.

The upshot of all this is that Askar, finally, is himself part of that quasi-incestuous abuse of power which in the novel is a symptom and hallmark of the narrow, introverted ethnocentrism that prevents the Somalis from opening up, hospitably, to neighbouring cultures. In the book's allegoric scheme, Askar represents a chauvinistic Somali concept of the Ogaden as his real mother represents the dead dream of an ethnic nation, of "Mother Somalia" as the Ogaden's natural parent, "getting together" with "the Ogaden/child separated from her" (p. 97). Misra signifies a broader, hybrid, generic concept of the Ogaden, in which mixed ethnicity is metaphorically indexed to sexual indeterminacy, and her hybridization signifies everything that he must destroy to realize his sectarian Somali dreams. "One day [...] you will identify yourself with your people and identify me out of your community," she prophesies, "you might even kill me to make your people's dreams become a tangible reality" (p. 95). What Askar, self-laceratingly, attempts is tantamount to these things. Together with his uncles, he "others" Misra, misogynistically and xenophobically, as woman and foreigner, as a sexual and political territory to be invaded and colonized; and this separative process, even as it unstabilizes roles in the parent-child relationship, reaffirms gender lines, making them as rigidly divisive as the nationality categories on the Somali maps with which they are aligned (as in "male" Ogaden and "female" Somalia). Askar, for all his androgynous fantasies, has undergone a typical, traditional Ogadenese upbringing in which male and female roles are strictly differentiated, and he is initially deeply disturbed by Hilaal and Salaado's confounding of traditional gender roles. For a viable concept of the nation to be created, it must first, it seems, be neutered; for the nation to be successfully *en*gendered, it must first be *un*gendered.

Askar remains torn by conflicting impulses, but his desire to exorcize Misra's presence from himself ultimately appears to outdo his desire to be at one with her; his assertive, separate male self quells his fears of the sexually indefinite. In the allegoric scheme, this means that the desire that the Ogaden should fulfil a specifically Somali destiny overrides considerations of cultural pluralism and interpenetration. "So long as I lived, she would too," Askar notes of his and Misra's symbiotic lives and, by extension, of the national groupings with which they are entangled (p. 37). But, as Salaado observes, wars, like the maps they are fought over, kill "trust and interdependence" (p. 53). As presented through the psychology of Askar, the Ogaden's cultural hybridization, like the androgynous interplay with which it is metaphorically correlated in the novel, exists in a state of thwarted potential, not as an achieved reality.

In an article on cartographic decolonization published just before the disintegration and re-ethnification of Central Europe, Graham Huggan speculated optimistically about the potential capacity of contemporary postcolonial writing (particularly Australian and Canadian writing) to challenge the homogeneity of ethnocentric colonial discourses.[17] The business of the counter-discourses, he suggested, was to project spaces other than, or to articulate spaces between, those inscribed on the hegemonic map. These resistive, "deterritorializing" readings, according to Huggan, celebrate the diversity and mixed ethnicity of formerly colonized cultures, previously ignored or stigmatized by the dominant colonial one, and indicate a shift away from cultural homogeneity. The revised rhetorical spaces, he noted, may be "occupied by feminism, regionalism and ethnicity," each of them a counter-discursive strategy which "avoids circumscription within one or other form of cultural centrism."[18] A novel written in the spirit of such a strategy, published three years after Huggan's article, is *The English Patient* by the Sri Lankan-born Canadian writer Michael Ondaatje. Ondaatje's Hungarian map-maker, a man of no and any identity, speaks for a cosmopolitan cast of English, Canadians, Indians and Italians in North Africa during the Second World War:

> We were German, English, Hungarian, African [...] Gradually we became nationless. I came to hate nations. We are deformed by nation-states. The desert could not be claimed or owned - it was a piece of cloth carried by winds, never held down by stones, and given a hundred shifting names [...] By the time the war arrived, after ten years in the desert, it was easy for me to slip across borders, not to belong to anyone, to any nation. [...] I believe in such cartography - to be marked by nature, not just to label ourselves on a map like the names of rich men and women on buildings. We are communal histories, communal books. We are not owned or monogamous in our taste and experience. All I desired was to walk upon such an earth that had no maps.[19]

Unhappily - and it is the cause of much lamentation within the novel - there are no such countering and liberalizing energies at work in the contemporary Africa of *Maps*. Farah's indigenous desert world is a far cry from Ondaatje's expatriate one and perhaps has a stronger, and sadder, claim to historical authenticity. In *Maps* the new dominant (and *re*territorializing) discourses are themselves insularly and oppressively ethnic. Ethnicity and ethnic nationalism are here the hegemonic powers, not the revisioning agents: the regional map is the instrument of new, postcolonial ethnocentrisms and false cultural homogeneities forced upon a hybridized reality. Africa's internal imperialisms have taken over from where the alien, external ones left off. Farah's novel offers us new maps for old. Insofar as it anticipates the re-ethnification trends of the 1990s, it also offers us a map of the modern world.

CHAPTER EIGHT
Donors and Foundlings: *Gifts*

Farah, a writer who refers constantly in interviews to work in progress and completed manuscripts placed with literary agents, first announced the imminent publication of his novel *Gifts* in 1986, shortly after the appearance of *Maps*. Readers then had to wait (surprisingly, for a prolific novelist who had published six novels in fifteen years), until 1992 for the book's African publication, by a Zimbabwean press, and for its subsequent British distribution - a postponement which may have had something to do with the desire to publish in Africa before releasing the book world wide. *Gifts* appears to have had an indecisive gestation, its final version having shifted somewhat from its original conception. In the 1986 interview, and again in a 1988 essay, the novelist spoke of the book as being the second part of "a carefully planned trilogy" of novels with *Maps* as the first volume and a novel variously titled *Motives* and *Letters* as the third.[1] It came as some surprise, therefore, when the new book, like the one before it, started afresh with a completely new cast of characters, particularly to readers accustomed to the "transworld" identities, reappearing in novel after novel, of the characters in the earlier work. *Gifts*, moreover, appears to have no obvious thematic, historical or stylistic connection with *Maps* and there is little evidence that it is part of a second trilogy of novels.

The Somalia of *Gifts* is not yet the catastrophe-stricken, aid-inundated nation of 1990s newsreels, but the Mogadiscio depicted in the novel is closer to the post-Barre breakdown than the city presented in *Maps*, and there are signs enough of the coming chaos. Houses are Yale-locked against burglars, motorists loiter at roundabouts intent on ambush or rape, scuffles break out on streets lined with beggars and scarce of cars. Already there are food shortages, galloping inflation and a rampant black market. Transport and medical services, basic amenities and energy supplies are running down: "No electricity, no water, no baked bread, no papers."[2] When the power fails the "privilegentzia" switch on their portable generators, but the hospital nurse and midwife who is the central character in the novel lives on the boundary of this class, in one of the few houses in the poor district that still have running water and toilet facilities. *Gifts*, however, is not about a society breaking down. "All stories are one story, whose principal theme is love," says the heroine's benefactor-brother on the last page: the novel is, first and foremost, a love story.

Gifts tells the story of Duniya, a twice-married 35-year old single parent, and the process by which she slowly succumbs to the loving gift-offerings of the widowed Bosaaso, a United Nations worker recently returned from America. When she begins to spill and upset things in the hospital ward Duniya reflects that in Somali mythology the cosmos is balanced on the horns of a bull and earthquakes are caused whenever his love, the cow, turns her gaze elsewhere. In other words, love is the force that holds the universe in equilibrium, and Duniya, whose name means "world" or "cosmos," loses her balance when she refuses to acknowledge that she has been affected by it. Duniya has known only marriage, not love, so when it comes knocking for the first time, it knocks her over and she finds herself also "tripping and knocking things over in clumsy gestures of lost equilibrium" (p. 104). Duniya is that familiar figure in Farah's fiction: the much-married Somali woman imprisoned by patriarchal Islamic tradition, her position negotiated by men. At the outset of her marital career she is herself a "gifted" property, given by her father in a customary marriage to his friend, the blind Zubair, a man who is three times her age and who made her the gift of a horse when she was a child. One of the subsequent "givens" of her destiny is to be controlled by the uncles, brothers, half-brothers and husbands whose charge she is and in whose houses she is temporarily accommodated:

> The landmarks of her journey through life from infancy to adulthood were marked by various 'stations,' all of them owned by men, run and dominated by men. [...] A homeless woman is one who has no husband or a male relation to provide her with shelter. (pp. 171, 173).

Woman, in Somali society, is a homeless person, property-less because she is herself a property. Duniya moves from her father's house into her ageing husband's and from there into a tenancy to the journalist-landlord Taariq, who makes her his live-in companion and then his wife, but turns out to be a drunken and demanding husband. After the divorce from Taariq she takes a tenancy for a while to her petulant half-brother Shiriye, under whose rule she and her twin-children live "in virtual terror and humiliation," and then another, almost rent-free tenancy to her full-brother Qaasim - until she quarrels with his wife Muraayo and effectively serves a quit-notice on herself. With the practical help of Bosaaso and the aid of three thousand U.S.dollars from her rich expatriated brother Abshir, she finally secures a city-centre flat, but even this alternative pied-a-terre provided by the "omnipresent, benevolent, well-meaning" Abshir to help her preserve her independence is but another male gift. And as gifts have conditions and built-in dependencies, Duniya has grown wary and distrustful of them and has cultivated a habit of looking them in the mouth. She puts up a determined resistance to unauthorized donations of food or money brought home by her children from aunts, uncles and stepfathers, and from the opening scene, in which she unwittingly accepts a compromising lift from Bosaaso, disguised as a taxi driver, she remains suspicious of her suitor's attentions, his money and his American Green Card: "Unasked-for generosity has a way of making one feel obliged, trapped in a labyrinth of dependence. [...] I hate it when men take me for granted, as a woman" (pp. 20, 89).

Duniya's personal story is foregrounded, however, against a larger social and political canvas and opens out into the wider perspective of international gifts from first to third world countries, each chapter ending with a newspaper snippet about American and United Nations aid to famine-stricken nations in the Horn and other parts of Africa. As the fable unfolds, Farah explores the complex psychology of donorship, its binding ties and dependencies and the ways in which they change the relationship between giver and receiver; in the course of his inquiry he addresses the perennial problems of when and how to give and to receive, and the more fundamental question of - in Taariq's words - "who gets what, gives what to whom?"

In one of the novel's flashbacks the crass Danish voluntary aid worker Ingrid tells Bosaaso's late wife Yussur: "Aid is aid, good or bad, whether there are strings attached and whatever its terms of reference" (p. 46). But this is not so. Aid, at whatever level, is a moveable and variable feast. Political gifts to nations, like personal gifts to people, bind together donor and recipient in a variety of ways, and may be given with the best and worst of motives and results. Gifts may enable or enslave, motivate or humiliate. They can express affection, compassion, loyalty or penance, or assert superiority and dominance. They may angle to get something in return, in the hope (though hardly in the case of Africa) that yesterday's recipients will become tomorrow's donors, or, like the surplus food rotting in Taariq's freezer during power cuts, may merely express the desire to get rid of what the owner no longer has any use for. Gifts may be offered freely and selflessly, without conditions, like the unpaid services which the indigenous donors Bosaaso and Dr Mire render on returning to their country - a "giving for its own sake," free of worldly vainglory and without reference to Protestant salvationist ethics or the heavenly rewards of Judaic and Islamic systems (Somalis, says Mire, "defer to death" and hope for no such dividends; pp. 45, 93). Or they may be given as a bribe to buy passive co-operation or consent, like the bride-gifts that Shiriye secretly accepts from Zubair at the latter's marriage to Duniya. Even Duniya, who reviles such use of gifts, employs them in like fashion, bribing her nine-year-old daughter Yarey with promises of videos and Walkmans to quell her impetuous demands to be allowed to return to the maternal home. Alternatively, aid may carry hidden investments and returns, like the secondment of Italian professors to the Somali National University to maintain the imperial language and culture in the ex-colony, or the American food-aid programmes which enable American expatriates, in Yussur's words, to "live like lords in luxury they are not used to at home" (pp. 96-97, 47). Such aid is no more a gift than the third-hand china that Ingrid sells "dirt cheap" to Bosaaso, since, as with the china, Somalis end up paying a price for it in one way or another. "Some gifts," says Sagal in *Sardines*, "humiliate the receiver while they edify the donor,"[3] and these self-interested international donations fall into that category.

The effects of gifts are as mixed as the motives behind them. Gifts may energize or enervate, begetting industry or inertia. They can be constructive of new freedoms but may also create abject dependencies, and Bosaaso, the United Nations worker, has experienced both in his personal, as in his professional, life. In the first category is his purchase, in his own name, of a taxi for a poor cousin to earn an income from: this act, like Abshir's $3,000 gift to secure and convert Duniya's city-centre flat, stimulates activity and promotes self-help and self-reliance. In the second, negative category is his payment of his in-law's bills after his wife's death, an excessive generosity which breeds a parasitic dependence in his sister-in-law Waaberi and, like IMF loans to Mercedes-driving African government-elites, encourages her to live recklessly beyond her means (similarly, Aunt Muraayo makes Duniya's young daughter Yarey dependent upon herself by an addictive supply of videos). Waaberi has, finally, to curb her self-indulgence and, when Bosaaso flatly refuses to pay further accounts, is coerced into self-reliance, selling her jewellery to pay her electricity bills. Indiscriminate gifts may in fact be great evils, deathly or deadening in their effects, and they are, appropriately, attended in the novel by images of disease and decay: Duniya calls food gifts "corpse food," to be consumed only when the household provider is dead, and Bosaaso's mentally ill first wife throws her week-old baby over a balcony into the garden to fetch her the "gift" of a flower. The pernicious effects of such gifts are perhaps most strongly felt in the international context where unregulated, unevenly distributed aid may have murderous consequences. The moral of Taariq's newspaper article "The Story of a Cow," about a cow that insists on being milked by its owner's neighbours, is that Nature rewards those who share its gifts and nurture it, as "co-responsibles," on a communal and egalitarian basis, whether the gift be a cow or, as in this novel, a foundling child. But "foreign food donations," he observes in his later article "Giving and Receiving," "create a buffer zone between corrupt leaderships and the starving masses" (p. 194). Such gifts, as the news snippet on Ethiopia makes clear, prop up dictatorships by placing political weapons in their hands, endorsing "starve and rule" policies that deny food aid to rebels and dissidents. Famine, Taariq quotes Brecht, "is a trick up the powerful man's sleeve." Since shortages of both food at the national level and love at the domestic one are man-made, then the result of outside aid to remedy them may be the bolstering of corrupt power and influence, whether of an Ethiopian Emperor or a domestic patriarch.

"Every gift has a personality - that of its giver," writes Taariq. That personality may be modestly self-effacing, as in the case of the Chinese who build and run Mogadiscio's maternity hospital or of the old woman Maryam who refuses to acknowledge the hospitality she gave to the drunken, homeless journalist: "Why devalue the significance of the act by mentioning it in public?" (p. 124). In such cases, or where the gift is a communal one expressing a plurality of personalities, as in the Somali *Qaaraan*, the donors are virtually anonymous. In the context of international aid, however, this is seldom the case. Every foreign-donated sack of rice, notes Taariq, is stamped with "the characteristics and mentality of its donor" (p. 195). Not only does each gift carry the taint (sometimes literally, as with the Chernobyl-contaminated milk dumped on Africa) of a self-broadcasting, self-gratulatory media performance - promoted, significantly, in one of the book's UNICEF bulletins by a famous actress. More insidiously, with every piece of technological and educational aid come undesirable cultural by-products imported with the language and communications networks which are its mediums: for example, girls named after Hollywood actresses (Marilyn) and even after Western prophylactics and detergents ("Aasbro" and "Omo"). As Bosaaso's late wife, in a flashback, puts it to the aid worker

Ingrid, "a language is the product of a people's attitude to the world in which they find themselves" - and, one might add, to the rest of the world (p. 47). The recipient is expected to take over that gifted mentality, language and value-system and express his or her gratitude, whether to Uncle Sam (or Sung) or to the gift-laden Uncle Abshir, flying in from Rome like a rescuing angel at the end of the book with his pockets full of American dollars. The important difference in the case of Abshir's aid to Duniya, and the only thing that makes her continuing dependency upon him in any way acceptable, is that it is viewed not as a gift but as the repayment of a debt, as compensation for male mistreatment throughout her life. As Abshir puts it to her:

> If you were a boy, you wouldn't have been married off to a man as old as your grandfather in the first place, and in the second, you might have got a scholarship to a university of your choice, because you were brilliant and ambitious. An injustice has been done. It has been my intention to right the wrong as best I could. I am sorry. (p. 238)

Duniya is at last given her rightful dues as a woman and is paid out for the injustices done to her.

Gifts is an exquisitely patterned novel which moves deftly from microcosm to macrocosm, from the innermost recesses of the individual human heart to public catastrophe. Each chapter begins with a waking dream in the protagonal consciousness in which Duniya, or her representative in the dream, does unspecified damage to herself by spurning some gift brought by a bird or insect, often a butterfly or dragonfly which is repeatedly associated with the foundling child at the centre of the book. In one such dream a woman asleep under a tree rejects a hat and garland of leaves brought by a kestrel; in another, the bird brings her an illuminated disc which she destroys instead of accepting; in a third dream, an eagle ignores a gift of meat and attacks the giver. The narrative then proceeds inexorably outward to the media spectacle of international aid but does so through a series of personal and social "giftings." These include lifts to work and restaurant meals provided by Bosaaso, blood donations, rent-free tenancies, food parcels and, pivotal to the book, a symbolic present from Allah in the form of a baby purportedly found by Duniya's headstrong teenage daughter Nasiiba in a rubbish bin and brought home by her in the hope that it will cement her mother's relationship with Bosaaso (the child later turns out to be the illegitimate offspring of Duniya's brother Qaasim and Nasiiba's friend Fariid). Bridging the gap between the extremities, and personalising the public dimension, are strategically-placed mediatory scenes: for example, the one in which Bosaaso's late wife questions the motives of the Danish aid worker, and the scene in which Duniya quarrels with her brother's wife Muraayo. The latter appears to think that one of the conditions of Duniya's tenancy of Qaasim's house is her acceptance of the American toys, food and education which aunt and uncle force upon her daughter Yarey, to whom they are temporary guardians. As Duniya parodically puts it, "We can give you America and Canada on a tray and the world's T.V., video and toys at the push of a button" (p. 110). Farah's deft double-focus, however, is contrastive as well as comparative, concerned with points of both departure and convergence and carefully marking the limits of the parallels with important qualifications. Significantly, it is after reading Taariq's article on the dangers of international aid that Duniya decides to "make a gift of her body" to Bosaaso that night. Put crudely, Duniya needs Bosaaso's unexpected gifts and is able to receive them as an equal, without loss of pride, dignity and independence: Somalia may not need their political equivalents and is not in a position to accept them on the same terms (*Gifts* is written against the background of the 1984 Ethiopian famine, not the Somali crisis of the 1990s, though, arguably, the basic arguments about the political engineering of famine and misuse of aid still hold good).

At the structural centre of *Gifts* is the pivotal episode of the foundling child. Nasiiba's "Nameless One" attracts to Duniya's house a host of people, both well-wishers and doom-prophets, who, in their reactions to the foundling and their advice as regards what to do with it, express a range of attitudes towards the donation and reception of gifts at all levels. First comes Duniya's wretched half-brother Shiriye, a physically grotesque, disreputable fellow who has previously slandered her and stolen her share of the bride-wealth in both of her marriages, a man who has no understanding of kindness. Shiriye, predictably, utters only conventional petty moral indignation at his sister's taking in of a child who is almost certain to be illegitimate. Next comes Duniya's young daughter Yarey, who exults at the arrival of the child, "a foundling who made them all new friends" (p. 83). It is during Yarey's visit that there emerges the idea that the child has come with the purpose of forming the "central focus" of Duniya's and Bosaaso's affections and should be given to them because they would be the most fit and worthy parents, though it is also evident that they cannot yet provide the protective solidarity and security of marriage which the child needs. After Yarey comes her current guardian Muraayo, the feckless barren wife of Qaasim. Muraayo tries to exploit Duniya's dependent position as tenant and mother to blackmail her into handing over what she rightly suspects to be her own husband's bastard, whereupon Duniya promptly throws her out and gives up her tenancy. Next comes Duniya's ex-husband Taariq, whose role is to confer upon the child a mythic, symbolic identity: "everybody will get something different out of him" (p. 122). Farah's own voice is transparently close to the journalist's here[4] though, characteristically, he first allows the pragmatic Duniya to puncture the pretensions of the symbolism from within the narrative: "If something incurable kills him or if tetanus claims his life, will all this talk about myths have been mere babble, mere words, no more?" (p. 122). That this is not quite the case is apparent when the child, after a final stormy visit from its father Qaasim, suddenly dies and Duniya reflects: "Everybody had turned the foundling into what they thought they wanted, or lacked" (p. 128). The child is both catalyst and metaphor. It brings out the best and the worst in people, a living testimony to both Duniya's generosity and her relatives' meanness (for the father Qaasim it is merely "the little devil who has created so much discord"), and it acts as a symbolic index to their needs and inadequacies. Because it is their human failings, rather than their qualities, that finally prevail, the child - Allah's gift - is withdrawn: it dies, presumably, because none of the hosts or visitors are capable of receiving the gift in the way it is intended.

This death notwithstanding, *Gifts* is the most sunny and radiant, albeit not the most profound, of Farah's novels. Its gentle, teasing humour is a welcome relief after the dark menace and shrill psychological agonies of the *Dictatorship* trilogy, its disciplined clarity of style refreshing after the somewhat mannered esoterics of *Maps*. The characters of the quick-tempered, practical Duniya and the cool dignified intellectual Bosaaso, their tensions and tender love-making, are beautifully executed, and the novel abounds in delightful episodes: notably, Duniya's driving and swimming lessons, her exchanges with her precocious older daughter, and the satiric cameos of the worthless Shiriye and the embarrassing Muraayo. *Gifts* is Farah's first African-published book and it is clearly aimed, stylistically, at a broader and more African-based readership. For example, the learned epigraphic allusions to Western literature which open the chapters in the earlier books, and which some critics have found showy and pretentious, have been replaced by captions briefly summarizing the events that follow. This is a new, different Farah, interspersing his narrative with the familiar poetic dream-literature and oral folklore of Somali tradition but in a much more accessible form than hitherto.

Doubtless, Farah's critics will have some justifiable reservations about his latest novel. The foundling child dies just half-way through the book, too soon for it to be absolutely central but already invested with too much mytho-symbolic weight for it to bear in the limited space which it occupies in the book; when comparisons are made with Moses, Jesus and Sunjiata, one suspects that too much is being claimed for it. The gifts symbolism is similarly overdone. The word is used so often and in so many different contexts - Bosaaso's social-worker lover in America is "a gift," an out-patient's husband brings home the unwanted "gift" of gonorrhoea - that it threatens to become a verbal hold-all in which virtually anything can be put. And there are the usual vagaries of style, most conspicuous in the characters' conversational exchanges, where Somali idioms sound odd in their English renderings. Duniya exhorts Bosaaso to "cry from the loftiest minaret of your rage" and asks the shop-keeper how much she owes for "this blessed manna from the heavens of your kindness" (pp. 153, 160). Earlier in the book she reminds Nasiiba of the time when she lay asleep, her "cheeks tattooed with dried tear-stains" (p. 28). Such passages prompt the Western reader to ask if Somalis really speak in this high-flown poetic rhetoric, or are they merely made to talk as Farah writes? The problem is the perennial one of the "translated" author - a problem that the Westerner, without a knowledge of the indigenous language, cannot surmount.

Some foreseeable criticisms of the novel can, however, be answered or at least mitigated. The multiplication of new characters right up to the final chapters (such as Fariid and Abshir) inevitably diffuses the intensity with which the two central characters are focused: its point, however, is to keep widening the circle to take in extended family and community in both the national and (with Abshir's arrival from overseas) the international contexts. Inevitably, some critics will complain that the individual and national themes are not as consistently integrated, and the personal and public lives not as intricately interwoven as in the trilogy. In place of the subtle resonances of the latter work, we are apparently faced in the new novel with blocks of disparate material, and the leap from microcosm to macrocosm is sometimes too sudden and easy: as, for example, when Duniya explains her rejection of Bosaaso's dependency-forming gifts in terms of the Third World's need for self-reliance; or when the radio broadcast arbitrarily telescopes Somalia's foreign-aid requirements with the story of the baby found in the rubbish bin; or when the city's abandoned expatriate-owned dogs are compared with pampered African dictators deserted by their European sponsors. In *Gifts* the reader is presented with a series of imaginative leaps and twists, rather than a network of carefully worked-out logical correspondences, and there are moments when the symbolism seems to lapse into a kind of intellectual shorthand or telegraphese. But the book is finally, like all Farah's books, about individual members of families and the love between them, not a political tract or thesis. Essentially, the love story keeps stumbling upon surprising similarities with the international political situation which is its backdrop. If this is one of the book's weaknesses, it is one which is closely tied up with its strengths. The dovetailing of private and public themes is, admittedly, more enigmatic and less intense here than in Farah's other writing, but it is still informed by a boldly original metaphoric conception. *Gifts* is a poetically evocative as well as (politically) a mildly provocative work, and is full of unexpected echoes, startling insights and subtle quirks of characterization that will continue to surprise and delight his readers. Though not quite what was promised or expected, it was worth the six-year wait.

Somalia is a much-changed place since Farah left it in 1974. Twenty years on, the Mogadiscio which features in all his books is no more and one has to go back to novels like the early *A Naked Needle* to reconstruct it.[5] The city of ancient mosques and 900-year-old *Xamari* stone dwellings, terraced tea-houses and cosmopolitan restaurants, has been shelled and machine-gunned to rubble by the militias of the rival warlords in the civil war that followed the fall of Siyad Barre in May 1991. Thousands of Somalis have died in the famine produced by that war. Hundreds more have died, among them soldiers from Europe, Asia, America and other African countries, in the ill-prepared United Nations peace-keeping operation that accompanied the relief action. All of this, of course, post-dates the subject-matter of *Gifts*, written against the crises of the eighties, though Farah's publication in 1992 of yet another novel about Mogadiscio's Westernized "privilegentzia," amid media images of mass starvation in his country, will not endear him to his left-wing detractors. To them it will appear that he is writing about a country and a class that no longer exist.

In one sense, however, Farah has always written about a Somalia that no longer exists. His is the fiction of exile, drawing upon a store of memories of events, people and places that are no longer current, so there is an inevitable time-lag in all of his writing. The *Dictatorship* trilogy, most of which is set during the Soviet phase of Barre's rule, was completed in 1983, six years after Somalia's break with Russia over the Ogaden War. *Maps*, set during that war, appeared almost a decade after the event. It is merely that in *Gifts* the time-lag is more glaringly conspicuous because the book's subject has been overtaken, and its 1980s-view of famine dated, by the Somali national catastrophe and international media event of 1992-93. Though there are marginal references in the novel's radio and newspaper bulletins to massacres and food shortages in the "war-torn, drought-stricken north," war and anarchy are not yet a national condition and famine is conceived as a broad environmental disaster which is only partly man-made, the combined results of deforestation, over-grazing, locust-plagues, seasonal rainfall variations and intermittent military actions. Famine, as Taariq claims, may be "a trick up the powerful man's sleeve," but so - he neglects to say - is war, which produces the famine and which has played the principal part in the recent devastation in the Horn of Africa. Without foreknowledge of the coming cataclysm, Taariq is able in his journalism to take a surprisingly benign and optimistic view of famines, which are seen to "awake a people from an economic, social or political lethargy" and prompt them to overthrow their dictators (p. 194). Whether Siyad Barre's overthrow in 1991 and the ensuing political anomy were products or causes of the major famine remains open to dispute, however; and, as recent events have shown, mass-hunger only paralyzes and enfeebles populations, generating not revolutionary energy but despair. Famines do not so much arouse and unify nations as atomize them into chaos and confusion and, far from ousting corrupt rule, they place their people at the mercy of anarchic factions once rule has broken down.

In essay and interview statements Farah has generally presented his exile in a positive light, sometimes camouflaging his private pain with a bravura rhetoric to the effect that not he but the Somali people and its leadership are the ones really in exile, whether from modern history, their best selves or each other.[6] Perhaps making a virtue out of necessity, he has said that exile has given him not only physical safety but freedom to write without political pressures and family demands, along with the privacy and sense of self that are much-prized by a novelist born into a land of oral poets and fierce clan loyalties. In the case of nations ruled by despotic military juntas like the Somali one, it is better, he argues, to stay in physical exile outside the country than to suffer intellectual and spiritual exile inside it, silenced by censorship, bans or imprisonment; the physical exile is only a by-product of the intellectual one.[7] Farah also contends that "distance distils" and clarifies experience, and so is an aid to understanding.[8] But distance also, surely, estranges and alienates a writer from his native experience if it is maintained for too long a period and it poses a continuing dilemma to him, particularly when the main obstacle to repatriation - in Farah's case, Barre's dictatorship - has been removed. Farah has recently presented himself as a writer who is concerned with "challenging" as well as "representing" reality, admitting at the same time that he has been forced by the "special needs" of exile "to create an alternative reality."[9] However positive a light he throws upon his predicament, the problems of relevance and accuracy of representation must become especially acute in the career of a writer who continues to set his fiction in a homeland which he has not seen for twenty years. Farah, obviously aware of this, spoke in an earlier interview of living in a country of the mind, a country of his own imagination,[10] and, more recently, of having "written about a country bearing resemblances to Somalia."[11] Somalia, as it is currently situated, is no place for a writer to return to; but Somalia remains the source of Farah's inspiration as an artist and it now seems unlikely that he will set his novels in other parts of the world or in the other African countries where he has lived for the last decade. *Gifts*, because it is about the foreign aid of which famine relief makes up such a large part, leaves hanging the question of whether, and how, Farah will address the continuing plight of his country in the last years of this century. Farah has, of course, already dealt in his fiction with one of Somalia's national calamities, the Ogaden War, albeit in a highly idiosyncratic manner. It is doubtful, however, whether literature can contain or cope with catastrophes of the magnitude of the Somali crisis of the 1990s, or should even try: language chokes on the reality, art is helpless before its horror. Not surprisingly, Farah has recently abandoned the idea of writing a novel about the civil war and has embarked instead upon a non-fictional work on the experiences of Somali refugees in Europe: this is projected as "a study of the tragic conditions, the tragic side-products of the civil war."[12] Perhaps such subjects are unavailable to fiction and can be dealt with only in factual form.

Farah is an enigmatic figure, a writer whose next move is never easy to predict, but it is certain - whatever the future holds, and however he resolves the dilemmas of exile - that he has proved to be one of the most resilient, innovative and versatile of the post-war generation of African novelists. Over twenty years he has produced work in a rich variety of moulds, ranging from naive picaresque and sophisticated stream-of-consciousness narratives to political thrillers and dialectical novels of debate and, most recently, experimental fictions in the vein of the *bildungsroman* and the *roman-a-these*, set against the backdrops of war and international aid. Nuruddin Farah is now firmly established as a widely-respected and oft-quoted figure among African writers and intellectuals, and has left his mark on a younger generation of African novelists who are now coming into their own. Whatever happens in his homeland, it is clear that Farah will continue to write, and to produce fiction as exciting and adventurous as any being written on the African continent today. When the current documentary work is done, it will be intriguing to see in what direction and to what subject this remarkable novelist will next turn his prodigious literary gifts.

CHAPTER NOTES

Chapter 1

1 In Somalia surnames are not normally used. Persons are identified by their given name, followed by the name of their father and grandfather (the author's father was Hassan Farah). See B. W. Andrzejewski, "Somali Literature", in Bernth Lindfors (ed.), *Research Priorities in African Literature*. London & Munich: Hans Zell / K. G. Saur, 1984, p. 81.

2 In 1978 Somalia, with 92 % homogeneity, was ranked 28th in the world on a homogeneity-table of 135 nations. See "Somalia", in *Encyclopedia of the Third World*, Vol. 2. New York: Facts on File, 1978, p. 1303.

3 Nuruddin Farah, "Living in a Country of the Mind: Interview with Maggie Jonas", *New African* (December 1987), p. 61.

4 For my historical sketch of pre- and post-revolutionary Somalia in this chapter I have relied heavily on Chapters VII-X of I. M. Lewis, *A History of Modern Somalia: Nation and State in the Horn of Africa.* Revised & Expanded Edition; Boulder & London: Westview Press, 1988, pp. 139-266.
I have also consulted John Markakis, *National and Class Conflict in the Horn of Africa.* Cambridge: Cambridge University Press, 1987.

5 The revolutionary government's literacy campaign was largely an urban phenomenon. In 1978 the national literacy rate was still only 5 % and Somalia ranked 124th in the world on the literacy ratings: "Somalia", in *Encyclopedia of the Third World*, Vol. 2, p. 1310.

6 I. M. Lewis, *Religion in Context: Cults and Charisma.* Cambridge: Cambridge University Press, 1986, pp. 106-07.

7 In 1978 Somalia received a maximum negative rating of 7 in both political and civil rights on a descending scale from 1 to 7: *Encyclopedia of the Third World*, Vol. 2, p. 1304.

8 "I used to feel threatened most of the time in Somalia. I would be called every now and again after midnight to the Security for interrogation. I was arrested once or twice, it was very menacing." Farah, "Living in a Country of the Mind", p. 61.

9 Nuruddin Farah, "Why I Write", *Third World Quarterly* 10, 4 (1988), p. 1596.

10 Farah, "Why I Write", p. 1596.

11 Nuruddin Farah, "A Combining of Gifts: An Interview with Maya Jaggi", *Third World Quarterly* 11, 3 (1989), p. 183.

12 Nuruddin Farah, "Mapping the Psyche: An Interview with Robert Moss", *West Africa* (1 September 1986), p. 1827.

13 Nuruddin Farah, "Do Fences Have Sides?" in Uma Parameswaran (ed.), *The Commonwealth in Canada: Proceedings of the Second Triennial Conference of*

CACLALS, Part Two (University of Winnipeg, 1-4 October 1981). Calcutta: Writers' Workshop, 1983, pp. 179, 181.

14 Farah, "Mapping the Psyche", p. 1828.

15 Nuruddin Farah, "Interview with Armando Pajalich", *Kunapipi* 15, 1 (1993), p. 64.

16 See the following: B. W. Andrzejewski, "Somali Literature", in B. W. Andrzejewski, S. Pilaszewicz & W. Tyloch (eds.), *Literatures in African Languages: Theoretical Issues and Sample Surveys*. Cambridge: Cambridge University Press, 1985, p. 340; and Albert S. Gérard, *African Language Literatures: An Introduction to the Literary History of Sub-Sahara Africa*. Washington, D.C.: Three Continents Press, 1981, p. 169.

17 Farah, "A Combining of Gifts", p. 172.

18 Ali Jimale Ahmed notes that some sheikh-poets sabotaged the literacy campaign by the various subterfuges which they used to dissuade their people from learning to read; they were afraid that their power-monopolies, invested in the spoken word, would be eroded. Ali Jimale Ahmed, "Of Poets and Sheikhs: Somali Literature", in Kenneth Harrow (ed.), *Faces of Islam in African Literature*. James Currey / Heinemann, 1991, pp. 81-83.

19 Nuruddin Farah, "Childhood of My Schizophrenia", *The Times Literary Supplement* (23-29 November 1990), p. 1264.

20 Farah, "Why I Write", p. 1592.

21 Details of these traditional oral genres can be found in Andrzejewski, "Somali Literature", in Andrzejewski et al. (eds.), *Literatures in African Languages*, pp. 358-78; Andrzejewski, "Somali Literature", in Lindfors (ed.), *Research Priorities in African Literature*, pp. 75-76; and Ahmed, "Of Poets and Sheikhs", pp. 79-83.

22 Farah, "Mapping the Psyche", p. 1827; and "Interview with Armando Pajalich", p. 66.

23 See, for example, Peter Caracciolo, *The Arabian Nights in English Literature*. London: Macmillan, 1988, pp. xvii, 60-61.

24 Nuruddin Farah, "Committed Writer", *New African* (January 1979), p. 85.

25 See Brian McHale, *Postmodernist Fiction*. London: Methuen, 1987, pp. 57-58.

26 Ian Adam, "Nuruddin Farah and James Joyce: Some Issues of Intertextuality", *World Literature Written in English* 24, 1 (1984), pp. 41-42.

27 Nuruddin Farah, "Haunted Beauty of the New Uganda", *Weekend Guardian* (21-22 October 1989), p. 5.

28 Nuruddin Farah, "The Life and Death of Words", *South* (April 1984), p. 54.

29 Farah, "Interview with Armando Pajalich", p. 63.

30 Farah, "Mapping the Psyche", p. 1828.

31 Nuruddin Farah, *A Naked Needle*. London: Heinemann, 1976, p. 21.

32 Farah, "Why I Write", pp. 1597-98.

Chapter 2

1 Nuruddin Farah, *From A Crooked Rib*. London: Heinemann, 1970, p. 179. Further page references are given in parentheses in the text of the chapter.

2 The Koran says that both man and woman were created from "a single soul", not from a physical body. I am grateful to Betty Oliver for drawing my attention to this. *The Koran* 4: 1. Translated by N. J. Dawood, 1956; Fourth edition, Harmondsworth: Penguin, 1974, p. 366.

3 Florence Stratton, "The Novels of Nuruddin Farah", *World Literature Written in English* 25, 1 (1985), p. 25.

4 Amina H. Adan examines some Somali oral poems which challenge established prejudices by making precisely this point: that the horses and camels paid in bride-price to the woman's maiden family by her suitor should be considered as a kind of earned income and an economic contribution to that family. See Amina H. Adan, "Women and Words", *Ufahamu* 10, 3 (1981), p. 117.

5 See Theo Vincent (ed.), *Seventeen Black and African Writers on Literature and Life*. Lagos: Centre for Black and African Arts and Civilization, 1981, p. 48; Nuruddin Farah, "A View of Home from the Outside" (Interview with James Lampley), *Africa* 124 (December 1981), p. 81; and Ikhememho Okomilo, "Power Game in Somalia", *Africa* 101 (January 1980).

6 Nuruddin Farah, "A Combining of Gifts: An Interview with Maya Jaggi", *Third World Quarterly* 11, 3 (1989), pp. 176-77. Betty Oliver refers to these remarks by Farah in defence of Ebla's individualism in her M.A. thesis, "Patriarchy and Power: The Political Susceptibility of Islam in the Writing of Nuruddin Farah, with Particular Regard to the Position of Women", Northern Territory University, Darwin, 1991, pp. 20-21.

7 See, for example, D. R. Ewen, "Nuruddin Farah", in G. D. Killam (ed.), *The Writing of East and Central Africa*. London: Heinemann, 1984, p. 194.

8 See, for example: Jacqueline Bardolph, "Un cas singulier: Nuruddin Farah, écrivain somali", *Littératures Nationales* 85 (1986), p. 62; Rosemary Colmer, "Nuruddin Farah: Territories of Pain", in Robert Ross (ed.), *International Literature in English*. New York: Garland, 1991, p. 134; and Florence Stratton, "The Novels of Nuruddin Farah", p. 25. As a counterweight to high-minded allegorical readings of Ebla's marital misadventures, it is perhaps worth noting here that, in the Somali context, polyandry has more often been the subject of high farce and satiric comedy. In the popular play *Shabeelnaagood* (*Leopard Among the Women*) by Hassan Sheikh Mumin, performed at the National Theatre in Mogadiscio in 1968, a rogue-trickster ruins naive girls by repeatedly "marrying" them at bogus ceremonies performed by accomplices posing as sheiks. Ebla's situation bears some resemblance to that of the women in the play, which Farah would certainly have heard of even if he did not see it in performance. See Hassan Sheikh Mumin, *Leopard Among the Women: Shabeelnaagood - A Somali Play*. Translated by B. W. Andrzejewski. London: Oxford University Press, 1974.

9 Farah, "A Combining of Gifts", p. 180.

Chapter 3

1 Nuruddin Farah, *A Naked Needle*. London: Heinemann, 1976, p. 99. Further page references are given in parentheses in the text of the chapter.

2 *The Koran* 60: 10. Translated by N. J. Dawood, 1956; Fourth edition, Harmondsworth: Penguin, 1974, p. 268.

3 D. R. Ewen, "Nuruddin Farah", in G. D. Killam (ed.), *The Writing of East and Central Africa*. London: Heinemann, 1984, p. 199.

4 Ewen, p. 199.

5 Frantz Fanon, *Black Skin, White Masks*. Translated by Charles Lam Markmann. New York: Grove, 1961, p. 63.

6 David Beer, "Somali Literature in European Languages", *Horn of Africa* 2, 4 (1979): 34; "Nuruddin Farah: Committed Writer", *New African* (January 1979), p. 85.

Chapter 4

1 The three novels *Sweet and Sour Milk*, *Sardines* and *Close Sesame* together comprise the trilogy, *Variations on the Theme of an African Dictatorship* (referred to in the text as the *Dictatorship* trilogy).

2 Nuruddin Farah, *Sweet and Sour Milk*. London: Allison & Busby, 1979; Heinemann, 1980, p. 99. Page references are taken from the Heinemann edition and are given in parentheses in the text of the chapter.

3 The sense of uncertainty that Farah creates for his readers is enhanced by his withholding of information about the fate of his characters from one novel to the next, and when information is eventually released it may not even then be reliable. Exactly what happens to Loyaan is not clear, for in the next novel in the trilogy there is conflicting information about his fate: he is, variously, in prison and in forced exile. See Nuruddin Farah, *Sardines*. London: Heinemann, 1982, pp. 212, 241.

4 Nuruddin Farah, "Coming Out of Oral Tradition to Write about Dictatorship" (Interview with Mary Langille), *The Varsity* (University of Toronto), (26 November 1987), p. S7.

5 Nuruddin Farah, "Mapping the Psyche: An Interview with Robert Moss", *West Africa* (1 September 1986), p. 1827.

6 Farah, "Coming Out of Oral Tradition ...", p. S7.

7 Nuruddin Farah, *A Naked Needle*. London: Heinemann, 1976, p. 111.

8 Anne Walmsley, "Nuruddin Farah and Somalia", *Index on Censorship* 10, 2 (1981), p. 18.

9 Walmsley, p. 19.

10 D. R. Ewen, "Nuruddin Farah" in G. D. Killam (ed.), *The Writing of East and Central Africa*. London: Heinemann, 1984, p. 205.

11 Ian Adam, "The Murder of Soyaan Keynaan", *World Literature Written in English* 26, 2 (1986), pp. 209-10.

12 Jacqueline Bardolph, "*Yussuf and his Brothers* by Nuruddin Farah", *Commonwealth: Essays and Studies* 7, 1 (1984), p. 66.

13 Salman Rushdie, *The Satanic Verses*. London: Viking, 1988, p. 364.

14 Nuruddin Farah, *Sardines*. London: Heinemann, 1982, p. 78.

15 See Brian McHale, *Postmodernist Fiction*. London & New York: Methuen, 1987, pp. 33-34, 106-07.

16 Margaritta's polemic refers here to both the political and cultural expropriation of Africa by the imperial powers. Notoriously, Africa has occupied in the European imagination a conceptual rather than a geographical space, and has been mined by expatriate fiction for its multiple possibilities. It has served as a screen for the projection of imperial fantasies of adventure and exploration (Rider Haggard's romances), and as a void which is made simultaneously to absorb the intruder's imported nightmares and to provide him with an alibi for colonial occupation (Conrad's *Heart of Darkness*). More recently, Africa has been a playground for lexical improvisation (Walter Abish's *Alphabetical Africa*) and as parodic fodder for European fantasy-lore (Angela Carter's *The Infernal Desire Machines of Dr Hoffman*). McHale notes in his *Postmodern Fiction* (p. 54) that some of these writers have been troubled by an imperialism of the imagination which re-enacts the political zoning of the continent.

17 Nuruddin Farah, "Why I Write", *Third World Quarterly* 10, 4 (1988), p. 1597. Farah touches upon the General's theatrical habits again, through the main character Deeriye, in the third novel of the *Dictatorship* trilogy, *Close Sesame*: "Somalia has become a stage where the Grandest Actor performs in front of an applauding audience that should be booing him. Anyone who wishes to share the spotlight either goes mad or in the end is imprisoned. Otherwise, everyone is made to join the crowd and applaud with it." Nuruddin Farah, *Close Sesame*. London: Allison & Busby, 1983, p. 189.

18 Adam, p. 210.

19 Some of Farah's more laborious and inflated metaphors in *Sweet and Sour Milk* are hard to defend. For example, at the first meeting of Loyaan and Margaritta we are told that "an estuary of queries drowned whatever impressions she might have made on him" (p. 65), and Loyaan, at the outset of his quest, resolves puzzlingly to "gather and encounter the beginningless end of an afterbirth" (p. 102). The dialogue is also clumsily over-written in places, resulting in an artificial rhetoric which lacks a conversational ring. The secretary at the Registry Office, commenting on the lecherous designs of the new "tribal upstarts", refers casually to "fingers energised with the pushiness of lust" (p. 104), and Loyaan announces to Margaritta: "This drink is reaching my inhibited veins of Islamic puritanism and breaking down my defences" (p. 118).

20 Ewen, p. 202.

21 Ladan is a friend of Sagal, whom she thinks of telephoning on p. 51 of the novel, but neither Sagal nor anyone else mentions Ladan in *Sardines*. Her name is included twice on roll-calls of names in *Close Sesame*, but no information about her is provided: Farah, *Close Sesame*, pp. 106, 176.

22 In *Close Sesame* we learn that the street never gets to be named after Soyaan - another of the General's many broken promises: Farah, *Close Sesame*, p. 192.

Chapter 5

1 Nuruddin Farah, Interview with Alex Tetteh-Lartey about *Sweet and Sour Milk*, *BBC Arts and Africa* radio transcript 305 (1979).

2 Nuruddin Farah, *Sardines*. London: Allison & Busby, 1981; Heinemann, 1982, p. 250. Page references are taken from the Heinemann edition and are given in parentheses in the text of the chapter.

3 In Islamic tradition Mina is the site of Ibrahim's sacrifice of the ram in place of his son Ismael, or Ishmael. As Medina partly explains in the novel (*Sardines*, p. 146), Satan appeared to Ismael to warn him and offered three times to help him escape but was each time stoned by the boy. Today the three pillars, or *jamarat*, at Mina are ritually stoned by pilgrims to represent the stoning of Satan. See Cyril Glasse, *The Concise Encyclopaedia of Islam*. London: Stacey International, 1989, p. 270. Deeriye also refers to the practice of *rajiim*, the stoning of Satan at Mina, in the third part of the trilogy: Nuruddin Farah, *Close Sesame*. London: Allison & Busby, 1983, p. 58.

4 Patricia Alden, "New Women and Old Myths: Chinua Achebe's *Anthills of the Savannah* and Nuruddin Farah's *Sardines*", *Matatu* 8 (1991), p. 79.

5 Rosemary Colmer, "Nuruddin Farah: Territories of Pain", in Robert Ross (ed.), *International Literature in English*. New York: Garland, 1991, p. 138.

6 Alden, p. 79. Alden challenges my own reading of the episode of Nasser's and Dulman's arrests in my earlier article, "Parents and Power in Nuruddin Farah's *Dictatorship* trilogy", *Kunapipi* 11, 2 (1989), pp. 94-106. It is true that there is no supporting evidence in the narrative for Medina's direct involvement in the events. Nevertheless, in the Epilogue, immediately prior to Xaddia's entrance, Medina herself appears to claim responsibility, while showing little remorse, for the arrests. Drawing up a roll-call of the General's victims (Soyaan, Loyaan, Koschin, Siciliano, Nasser and Dulman) she asks when the terror began and, placing herself egotistically at the centre of events, asks: "Or should she begin with the day she moved out of the house, this being the very action which brought about all this?" (*Sardines*, p. 241). After the scene with Xaddia she reflects, "Heavy on her conscience were three persons - two of them dead and one as good as dead", though the identities of the three victims are not made clear: the reference may be to Soyaan, Siciliano and Koschin (*Sardines*, p. 249). When Deeriye, in the next book, informs the reader of Samater's imprisonment, he refers passingly to Medina's "self-afflicted paranoia": Farah, *Close Sesame*, p. 179.

7 Barbara Turfan, "Opposing Dictatorship: A Comment on Nuruddin Farah's *Variations on the Theme of an African Dictatorship*", *Journal of Commonwealth Literature* 24, 1 (1989), pp. 180-83.

8 Nuruddin Farah, "Mapping the Psyche: An Interview with Robert Moss", *West Africa* (1 September 1986), pp. 1827-28.

9 Gerald Moore, "Nomads and Feminists: The Novels of Nuruddin Farah", *International Fiction Review* 11, 1 (1984), p. 11.

10 Nuruddin Farah", Author in Search of an Identity: An Interview", *New African* (December 1981), p. 61.

11 Farah, "Mapping the Psyche", p. 1828.

12 *Sardines* is perhaps the most poetically intense of Farah's novels and the author's habit of tracking every quirk and dart of a character's consciousness in pursuit of its preoccupying tropes makes it a hard book to read through. There is a detailed analysis of the poetic structure of the novel in Jacqueline Bardolph, "Women and Metaphors in Nuruddin Farah's *Sweet and Sour Milk* and *Sardines*", in Thomas Labahn (ed.), *Proceedings of the Second International Congress of Somali Studies, University of Hamburg, 1-6 August 1983*. Hamburg: Helmut Buske Verlag, 1983, pp. 429-45.

13 Jung Chang, *Wild Swans: Three Daughters of China*. London: Flamingo, 1992, pp. 296, 298.

Chapter Six

1 Nuruddin Farah, *Sardines*. London: Heinemann, 1982, p. 240.

2 Nuruddin Farah, *Close Sesame*. London: Allison & Busby, 1983, p. 92.

3 It was Siyad Barre's general practice to find alternative ways of dealing with disaffected members of his own Mareehaan clan while summarily executing coup-plotters from other clans: for example, the seventeen officers of the Majerteen clan who attempted a coup in April 1978 after the Ogaden disaster. See Said S. Samater, "Oral Poetry and Political Dissent in Somali Society", *Ufahamu* 17, 2 (1989), p. 38.

4 Nuruddin Farah, "Interview with Armando Pajalich", *Kunapipi* 15, 1 (1993), p. 63. Considering the self-doubt and uncertainty in which he spends most of his time in the novel, Barbara Turfan's estimation of Deeriye as "a man who has come to terms with himself, who knows where he is and where he stands" sounds somewhat wide of the mark. Barbara Turfan, "Opposing Dictatorship: A Comment on Nuruddin Farah's *Variations on the Theme of an African Dictatorship*", *Journal of Commonwealth Literature* 24, 1 (1989), p. 177.

5 Omission has a negative retributive power in Somali Islam, expressed in the proverb "caado la burriyaa Caro Allay leedahay" (an abandoned custom brings forth the wrath of Allah). Ali Jimale Ahmed, "Of Poets and Sheikhs: Somali Literature", in Kenneth Harrow (ed.), *Faces of Islam in African Literature*. London: James Currey / Heinemann, 1991, p. 86.

6 Nuruddin Farah, "A Combining of Gifts: An Interview with Maya Jaggi", *Third World Quarterly* 11, 3 (1989), p. 185.

7 Ahmed, "Of Poets and Sheikhs", pp. 80, 88.

8 Farah, "A Combining of Gifts", p. 178.

9 Farah, "A Combining of Gifts", p. 182.

10 Samater, "Oral Poetry and Political Dissent", p. 35.

11 Ahmed, "Of Poets and Sheikhs", p. 84. The most famous of the Hurgumo poets of the 1981 Somali Salvation Democratic Front was a pan-Somalist named Khaliif, who used his verse for satiric attacks on the General's ruling Mareehaan clan. Samater, "Oral Poetry and Political Dissent", pp. 36-38.

12 By using the legendary Wiil-Waal's stories as touchstones for contemporary political issues and moral behaviour, Farah effectively closes the gap between what B. W. Andrzejewski has called the "time-bound" and "time-free" streams of Somali oral poetry. Traditionally, the topical political allusions of the former enjoy a higher prestige in Somali society than the myths and fables of the latter. B. W. Andrzejewski, "Somali Literature" in B. W. Andrzejewski, S. Pilaszewicz & W. Tyloch (eds.), *Literatures in African Languages: Theoretical Issues and Sample Surveys*. Cambridge: Cambridge University Press, 1985, pp. 368-69.

13 Andrzejewski, "Somali Literature", p. 343.

14 Sayyed Hassein Nasr, *Ideals and Realities of Islam*. London: Allen & Unwin, 1985, p. 18.

15 *The Holy Qur'an: Text, Translation & Commentary*, Vol. III., trans. Abdullah Yusef Ali. Lahore: Sh. Muhammad Ashraf, 1980, p. 1168. I am indebted to my doctoral student Maggi Phillips for drawing this to my attention. The theme of positive absence which I touch upon briefly in this chapter has been treated at greater length in her unpublished essay, "Sacred Breath and Diseased Word: Nuruddin Farah's *Close Sesame*", which is also a major component of her Ph.D. thesis on Farah, Head, Okri and others.

16 Jacqueline Bardolph, "Time and History in Nuruddin Farah's *Close Sesame*", *Journal of Commonwealth Literature* 24, 1 (1989), p. 203.

17 I. M. Lewis, *A Modern History of Somalia: Nation and State in the Horn of Africa*. 1965. Revised & Expanded Edition; Boulder & London: Westview Press, 1988, p. 77.

18 Bardolph, "Time and History", p. 196.

19 Said S. Samater, *Oral Poetry and Somali Nationalism*. Cambridge: Cambridge University Press, 1982, p. 8.

20 The historical details of the Sayyid period in this paragraph are taken from Lewis, *A Modern History of Somalia*, pp. 65-85.

21 In 1899 the British administration's colonial constabulary, the *Illalos*, attempted to incriminate the Sayyid by claiming that a bartered rifle was really stolen (Lewis,

p. 68). This is comparable with the General's invitation of Rooble to a clan meeting, only to arrest him for participating in an illegal assembly (*Close Sesame*, p. 104).

22 Said S. Samater reports that in June 1977 his tapes of the Sayyid's poetry were confiscated at Mogadiscio airport and almost led to his being detained; Samater, "Oral Poetry and Political Dissent", p. 32.

23 The messenger motif is affected by the doubleness that informs everything in this novel, being shaded both light and dark. The innocent deception of the eight-year-old Waris, whose intercepted message wreaks havoc in Deeriye's clan, is balanced by the benign misinformation of the nine-year-old Mursal who, by adding creatively to the messages he carries back and forth, contrives a happy marriage between two people who had no intention of entering into matrimony (*Close Sesame*, p. 192).

24 Fiona Sparrow, "Telling the Story Yet Again: Oral Traditions in Nuruddin Farah's Fiction", *Journal of Commonwealth Literature* 24, 1 (1989), p. 167.

25 Farah, "A Combining of Gifts", p. 181; "Interview with Armando Pajalich", p. 65.

26 Farah has said, apropos of Islamic condemnation of Naguib Mahfouz and Salman Rushdie: "For a Muslim believer, it is God who decides the destiny of all people; for a mortal to have a whip in his hand and to judge and determine the fate of someone in the name of the Lord is profoundly unIslamic" ("A Combining of Gifts", p. 182). The depoliticization of Islam has been taken up by reformist thinkers such as Fazlur Rahman in *Islam and Modernity: Transformation of an Intellectual Tradition* (Chicago: University of Chicago Press, 1982) and Akeel Bilgrami, "What Is a Muslim? Fundamental Commitment and Cultural Identity", *Critical Inquiry* 18 (Summer 1992), pp. 821-42. The pre-reformist, conservative position on Islam, based on the post-Medina verses and seeing it as pervading secular affairs, is represented by Nasr in *Ideals and Realities of Islam* (pp. 29-33). It has been observed that nomadic Muslims like the Somalis, though pious in their religious observances, were among the first to reject Islamic declarations in matters of social and political law: Albert S. Gérard, *African Language Literatures: An Introduction to the Literary History of Sub-Sahara Africa*. Washington, D.C.: Three Continents Press, 1981, p. 155.

27 Andrzejewski, "Somali Literature", p. 348.

28 Lewis, *A Modern History of Somalia*, pp. 81-84.

29 W. B. Yeats, *Collected Poems*, p. 280.

30 Farah has said that *Close Sesame* "is probably the one novel that will outlive all my other novels": "Interview with Armando Pajalich", p. 69.

Chapter Seven

1 Hilarie Kelly, "A Somali Tragedy of Political and Sexual Confusion: A Critical Analysis of Nuruddin Farah's *Maps*", *Ufahamu* 16, 2 (1988), pp. 21, 27, 29, 35.

2 Angela Smith, *East African Writing in English*. London: Macmillan, 1989, p. 40.

3 Jacqueline Bardolph, "*Maps* de Nuruddin Farah et l'Identité Somalie", *Bulletin des Etudes Africaines de l'INALCO* 7, 13-14 (1987), p. 252.

4 Rhonda Cobham, "Boundaries of the Nation: Boundaries of the Self: African Nationalist Fictions and Nuruddin Farah's *Maps*", *Research in African Literatures* 22, 2 (1991), pp. 94-95, 96.

5 Salman Rushdie, "In Good Faith" (1990) in his *Imaginary Homelands: Essays and Criticism 1981-1991*. London: Granta Books, 1991, p. 394.

6 Nuruddin Farah, *Maps*. London: Picador, 1986, p. 3. Further page references are given in parentheses in the text of the chapter.

7 A great deal of Somali oral poetry is, like the poet's fable in *Maps*, intricate and multi-layered, often using one ostensible order of experience to represent and disguise another, whether for artistic purposes or to evade political censorship. The she-camel is a traditional symbol of the nation in the oral tradition and during the Independence period has been used by both pre- and post-revolutionary poets (eg. Diriye Qaasim and Xaaji Aadan) to attack political maladministration. In one poem Aadan presents independent Somalia as a she-camel who is grossly neglected and starved by her herders, with the result that she can no longer give milk and is covered over with blood-sucking tics. The people rush to her rescue and are praised by the poet. In Farah's ironic version of the she-camel story, help comes too late and the rescuers aid her death. See B. W. Andrzejewski, "Somali Literature", in B. W. Andrzejewski, S. Pilaszewicz & W. Tyloch (eds.), *Literatures in African Languages: Theoretical Issues and Sample Surveys*. Cambridge: Cambridge University Press, 1985, pp. 360, 363, 367.

8 John S. Mbiti, *African Religions and Philosophy*. London: Heinemann, 1969, p. 110.

9 Susan Sontag, *Illness as Metaphor* and *Aids and Its Metaphors*. Harmondsworth: Penguin, 1991, pp. 47-50, 56-58, 65-69, 85-86.

10 Nuruddin Farah, "Childhood of My Schizophrenia", *Times Literary Supplement* (23 November 1990), p. 1264.

11 Nuruddin Farah, "Wretched Life: Interview with Patricia Morris", *Africa Events* (September 1986), p. 54. Askar's Pan-Somalism is a projection, albeit in extreme and jaundiced form, of Farah's own declared belief in the unity of all Somalis and their right to freedom of movement beyond both tribal and national frontiers: Nuruddin Farah, "A Combining of Gifts: An Interview with Maya Jaggi", *Third World Quarterly* 11, 3 (1989), pp. 175-76.

12 I. M. Lewis, *A Modern History of Somalia: Nation and State in the Horn of Africa*. 1965. Revised & Expanded Edition; Boulder & London: Westview Press, 1988, p. 11. Deeriye, in the previous novel, remembers the long lists of "ancestral names which he, as a child, had had to learn and recite to pay reverent reference to his clan's genealogy": Nuruddin Farah, *Close Sesame*. London: Allison & Busby, 1983, p. 49.

13 Nuruddin Farah, "Mapping the Psyche: Interview with Robert Moss", *West Africa* (1 September 1986), p. 1828.

14 Hussein A. Bulham, Review of *Maps*, *Africa Events* (July 1987), p. 79.

15 Cobham, "Boundaries of the Nation", pp. 89-90.

16 Cobham, "Boundaries of the Nation", p. 90.

17 Graham Huggan, "Decolonizing the Map: Post-Colonialism, Post-Structuralism and the Cartographic Connection", *ARIEL* 20, 4 (1989), pp. 115-31.

18 Huggan, "Decolonizing the Map", p. 127.

19 Michael Ondaatje, *The English Patient*. 1992. London: Picador, 1993, pp. 138-39, 261.

Chapter Eight

1 Nuruddin Farah, "Mapping the Psyche: An Interview with Robert Moss", *West Africa* (1 September 1986), p. 1827; Nuruddin Farah, "Why I Write", *Third World Quarterly* 10, 4 (1988), p. 1599. More recently, Farah has given this third novel the title *Secrets*: Nuruddin Farah, "Interview with Armando Pajalich", *Kunapipi* 15, 1 (1993), p. 69.

2 Nuruddin Farah, *Gifts*. Harare: Baobab; London: Serif, 1992, p. 17. Further page references are given in parentheses in the text of the chapter.

3 Nuruddin Farah, *Sardines*. London: Heinemann, p. 230.

4 Farah said in the 1986 interview: "I lost control over a character in *Gifts*, who behaved in the most rebellious manner." Taariq would seem to be the likeliest contender for this comment. "Mapping the Psyche", p. 1827.

5 Putting a brave face on the city's destruction, Farah has said in a recent interview: "One of the things that also in a sense I am very happy about is that in a novel like *A Naked Needle* there is a description of many parts of Mogadiscio, street by street, so that the real Mogadiscio today fades in comparison to the written-about Mogadiscio and so if somebody wants to reconstruct Mogadiscio today one may read *A Naked Needle* and see what street was called what, and what it looked like." Farah, "Interview with Armando Pajalich", p. 63.

6 Nuruddin Farah, "Living in a Country of the Mind: Interview with Maggie Jonas", *New African*, (December 1987), p. 61; Nuruddin Farah, "A Combining of Gifts: An Interview with Maya Jaggi", *Third World Quarterly* 11, 3 (1989), p. 183.

7 Nuruddin Farah, "Do Fences Have Sides?", in Uma Parameswaran (ed.), *The Commonwealth in Canada: Proceedings of the Second Triennial Conference of CACLALS, Part Two* (University of Winnipeg), 1-4 October 1981. Calcutta: Writer Workshop, 1983, pp. 176-77.

8 Farah, "Living in a Country of the Mind", p. 60.

9 Farah, "Interview with Armando Pajalich", pp. 61, 71.

10 Farah, "Living in a Country of the Mind", p. 61.

11 Farah, "Interview with Armando Pajalich", p. 61.

12 Farah, "Interview with Armando Pajalich", p. 70.

BIBLIOGRAPHY
Works by Nuruddin Farah

Novels

From A Crooked Rib. London: Heinemann, 1970.

A Naked Needle. London: Heinemann, 1976.

Sweet and Sour Milk. London: Allison & Busby, 1979; London: Heinemann, 1980; Saint Paul, Minnesota: Graywolf Press, 1992.

Sardines. London: Allison & Busby, 1981; London: Heinemann, 1982; Saint Paul, Minnesota: Graywolf Press, 1992.

Close Sesame. London: Allison & Busby, 1983; Saint Paul, Minnesota: Graywolf Press, 1992.

Maps. London: Picador, 1986.

Gifts. Harare: Baobab Books; London: Serif Publishers, 1992.

Essays

"Do You Speak German?" *Okike* 22 (1982), p. 33-38.

"Do Fences Have Sides?" In Uma Parameswaran (ed.), *The Commonwealth in Canada: Proceedings of the Second Triennial Conference of CACLALS, Part Two* (Conference held at University of Winnepeg, 1-4 October 1981). Calcutta: Writers' Workshop, 1983, pp. 174-82.

"The Creative Writer and the African Politician." *Nigerian Guardian* (7 September 1983), p. 11; *Classic* 1 (1984), pp. 27-30.

"The Life and Death of Words." *South* (April 1984), p. 54.

"A Tale of Tyranny" (review of Chinua Achebe's *Anthills of the Savannah*). *West Africa* (21 September 1987), pp. 1828-31.

"Why I Write." *Third World Quarterly* 10, 4 (1988), pp. 1591-99.

"Teutonic Aggro." *West Africa* (7-13 August 1989), p. 1292.

"Haunted Beauty of the New Uganda." *Weekend Guardian* (21-22 October 1989), p. 5.

"Childhood of My Schizophrenia." *The Times Literary Supplement* (November 23-29, 1990), p. 1264.

"Fear is a Goat." *The Guardian* (Lagos) 1 June 1990.

Interview

Anon. "Nuruddin Farah - Committed Writer." *New African* (January 1979), p. 85.

Anon. "*Close Sesame*: The End of a Trilogy." *Africa Now* (December 1983), pp. 82-83.

Anon. "Just Talking: Chinua Achebe and Nuruddin Farah." *Artrage* 14 (Autumn 1986), pp. 4-8.

Aiyejina, Funso, and Bob Fox. "Nuruddin Farah in Conversation with Funso Aiyejina and Bob Fox." *Ife Studies in African Literature and the Arts* 2 (1984), pp. 24-37.

Caulker, Elaine. "Interview with Nuruddin Farah about his Writing." *BBC Arts and Africa* radio transcript 47 (1974), pp. 3-4.

Frederikse, Julie. "Interview with Nuruddin Farah." *BBC Arts and Africa* radio transcript 506 (1983), p. 1-5.

Imfeld, Al. "Nuruddin Farah." In *African Writers On the Air*. Cologne: DW Dokumente, Deutschlandfunk Dokumentation & Archive, 1983-84, pp. 112-19.

Jaggi, Maya. "A Combining of Gifts: An Interview." *Third World Quarterly* 11, 3 (1989), pp. 171-87.

Jonas, Maggie. "Living in a Country of the Mind." *New African* (December 1987), pp. 60-61.

Kitchener, Julie. "Author in Search of an Identity." *New African* (December 1981), p. 61.

Lampley, James. "A View of Home from the Outside." *Africa* (December 1981), pp. 81-82.

Langille, Mary. "Coming Out of Oral Tradition to Write about Dictatorship." *The Varsity* (University of Toronto), (26 November 1987), p. S7.

Marshall, Julian. "Interview with Nuruddin Farah about his play *The Offering*." *BBC Arts and Africa* radio transcript 109 (1976), pp. 4-5.

Morris, Patricia. "Interview: Nuruddin Farah in London." *African Concord* (24 April 1986), p. 40.

----------. "Wretched Life." *Africa Events* (September 1986), pp. 54-55.

Moss, Robert. "Mapping the Psyche." *West Africa* (1 September 1986) pp. 1827-28.

Nazareth, H. O. "In the Land of the General." *City Limits* (11 November 1983).

Okezie, Emmanuel. "The Novel Form is not African: Nuruddin Farah Speaks on Writing in Africa in a Common Language." *This Week* (13 October 1986), p. 39.

Pajalich, Armando. "Nuruddin Farah Interviewed by Armando Pajalich." *Kunapipi* 15, 1 (1993), pp. 61-71.

Sweetman, David. "Interview with Nuruddin Farah." *BBC Arts and Africa* radio transcript 355 (1980), pp. 1-6.

Tetteh-Lartey, Alex. "Interview with Nuruddin Farah about BBC Somali Short Competition he adjudicated." *BBC Arts and Africa* radio transcript 67 (1975), pp. 1-3.

----------. "Interview with Nuruddin Farah." *BBC Arts and Africa* radio transcript 100 (1975), pp. 1-6.

----------. "Interview with Nuruddin Farah about *Sweet and Sour Milk*." *BBC Arts and Africa* radio transcript 305 (1979), pp. 1-5.

----------. "Interview with Nuruddin Farah about his Trilogy of Novels, especially *Close Sesame*." *BBC Arts and Africa* radio transcript 519 (1983), pp. 3-5.

Vaughan, P. & R. Wells. "Kaleidoscope." *BBC Arts* radio discussion of Farah's works, especially *Maps*. Radio transcript (13 March 1986), pp. 5-7.

Vincent, Theo. "Nuruddin Farah, Somalia." In Theo Vincent (ed.), *Seventeen Black And African Writers on Literature and Life*. Lagos: Centre for Black and African Arts and Civilization, 1981, pp. 111-19.

Vivan, Itala. "Letteratura Somala: Anatomia di una dittatura." *Nigrizia* (December 1984), pp. 42-43.

Unpublished Works

Why Dead So Soon? (novella), serialized in *Somali News*, Mogadiscio, 1966; not available in any other published form.

Doctor and Physicist (revue), broadcast on Indian radio, 1968.

A Dagger in Vaccuum (play), 1969; not produced.

Tolow Waa Talee Ma (extract from novel in Somali), printed in *Somali News*, Mogadiscio, 1973; serial publication censored and discontinued.

The Offering (play), written in lieu of thesis for uncompleted M.A. course, University of Essex, 1976; not submitted or produced.

A Spread of Butter (play), broadcast by BBC African Service, 24 December 1978.

Yussuf and His Brothers (play), produced at University of Jos, Nigeria, 2-4 July 1982.

Other Works

Adam, Ian. "Aesthetically Radical Fiction" (review of *Sardines*). *CRNLE Reviews Journal* 1 (1983), pp. 91-93.

----------. "Nuruddin Farah and James Joyce: Some Issues of Intertextuality." *World Literature Written in English* 24, 1 (1984), pp. 34-42.

----------. Review of *Close Sesame*. *World Literature Written in English* 24, 2 (1984), pp. 250-52.

----------. "The Murder of Soyaan Keynaan." *World Literature Written in English* 26, 2 (1986), pp. 203-11.

Adan, Amina H. "Women and Words." *Ufahamu* 10, 3 (1981), pp. 115-42.

Ahmed, Ali Jimale. "Of Poets and Sheikhs: Somali Literature." In Kenneth Harrow (ed.), *Faces of Islam in African Literature*. London: James Currey / Heinemann, 1991, pp. 79-89.

Ahmed, Christine Choi. "God, Anti-Colonialism and Drums: Sheikh Unways and the Uwaysiyya." *Ufahamu* 17, 2 (1989), pp. 96-117.

Alden, Patricia. "New Women and Old Myths: Chinua Achebe's *Anthills of the Savannah* and Nuruddin Farah's *Sardines*." *Matatu* 8 (1991), pp. 67-80.

Alrawi, Karim. "Nuruddin Farah: Webs of Intrigue." *New African* (June 1987), pp. 12-13.

Andrzejewski, B. W. & I. M. Lewis. *Somali Poetry: An Introduction*. London: Oxford University Press, 1964.

Andrzejewski, B. W. "Somali Literature." In Bernth Lindfors (ed.), *Research Priorities in African Literature*. London & Munich: Hans Zell / Saur, 1984, pp. 75-85.

----------. "Somali Literature." In B. W. Andrzejewski, S. Pilaszewicz & W. Tyloch (eds.), *Literatures in African Languages: Theoretical Issues and Sample Surveys*. Cambridge: Cambridge University Press, 1985, pp. 368-69.

Balogun, Françoise. "Promenade à travers les romans de Nuruddin Farah." *Présence Africaine* 145 (1988), pp. 157-64.

Bardolph, Jacqueline. "Women and Metaphors in Nuruddin Farah's *Sweet and Sour Milk* and *Sardines*." In Thomas Labahn (ed.), *Proceedings of the Second International Conference of Somali Studies 1-6 August 1983*. Hamburg: Buske, 1984, pp. 429-45.

----------. "Yussuf and His Brothers by Nuruddin Farah." *Commonwealth: Essays and Studies* 7, 1 (1984), pp. 57-70.

----------. "Un cas singulier: Nuruddin Farah, écrivain somali." *Notre Librairie* 85 (1986), pp. 61-64.

----------. "L'évolution de l'écriture dans la trilogie de Nuruddin Farah: Variations sur le thème d'une dictature africaine." *Nouvelles du Sud* 6-7 (1986-87), pp. 79-91.

----------. "*Maps* de Nuruddin Farah et l'Identité Somalie." *Bulletin des Etudes Africaines de l'INALCO* 7, 13-14 (1987), pp. 249-66.

----------. "Time and History in Nuruddin Farah's *Close Sesame*." *Journal of Commonwealth Literature* 24, 1 (1989), pp. 193-206.

----------. "Idéologie et fiction chez Ngugi Wa Thiong'o et Nuruddin Farah." *Notre Librairie* 98 (1989), pp. 88-92.

----------. "Nuruddin Farah." In Bernth Lindfors & Reinhard Sander (eds.), *Dictionary of Literary Biography: Twentieth Century Caribbean & Black African Writers*, Vol. 123. Detroit: Gale Research, 1993, pp. 35-40.

Beer, David. "Aspects of Somali Literature in European Languages." *Horn of Africa* 2, 4 (1979), pp. 27-35; reprinted as "Somalia" in Albert Gérard (ed.), *European Language Writing in Sub-Saharan Africa, Vol. 2*. Budapest: Akademiai Kiado, 1986, pp. 999-1010.

----------. "Nuruddin Farah." In Leonard S. Klein (ed.), *Encyclopedia of World Literature in the Twentieth Century*. New York: Frederick Ungar, (1982), pp. 76-77.

Bilgrami, Akeel. "What is a Muslim? Fundamental Commitment and Cultural Identity." *Critical Inquiry* 18 (Summer 1992), pp. 821-42.

Breitinger, Eckhard. "Experiments in the Novel Form: Soyinka, Farah, Ngugi, Fugard." In Eckhard Breitinger & Reinhard Sander (eds.), *Studies in Commonwealth Literature: Papers Presented at the Commonwealth Literature & Language Conference at Bayreuth University, June 16-19, 1983*. Tübingen: Gunter Narr, 1985, pp. 95-104.

Bulham, Hussein A. Review of *Maps*. *Africa Events* (July 1987), pp. 78-79.

Cahill, Kevin. *Somalia: A Perspective*. Albany: State University of New York Press, 1980.

Calder, Angus. "Sweet and Sour" (review of *Sweet and Sour Milk*). *The Literary Review* 8-21 March 1980, p. 13.

----------. "Nachbemerkung." In Nuruddin Farah, *Aus Einer Rippe Gebaut* (*From a Crooked Rib*). Translated by Gunter Bohnke. Bonnheim-Merten: Lamuv, 1986, pp. 134-38.

Caracciolo, Peter L. (ed.). *The Arabian Nights in English Literature*. London: Macmillan, 1988.

Chang, Jung. *Wild Swans: Three Daughters of China*. London: Flamingo, 1992.

Cobham, Rhonda. "Boundaries of the Nation, Boundaries of the Self: African Nationalist Fictions and Nuruddin Farah's *Maps*." *Research in African Literatures* 22, 2 (1991), pp. 83-98. Reprinted in expanded form as "Misgendering the Nation: African Nationalist Fictions and Nuruddin Farah's *Maps*" in Andrew Parker (ed.), *Nationalisms and Sexualities*. New York: Routledge, 1992, pp. 42-59.

Cochrane, Judith. "The Theme of Sacrifice in the Novels of Nuruddin Farah." *World Literature Written in English* 18 (1979), pp. 69-77.

Colmer, Rosemary. "Nuruddin Farah: Territories of Pain." In Robert Ross (ed.), *International Literature in English*. New York: Garland, 1991, pp. 131-42.

Crace, Jim. "Drowning in Style" (review of *Close Sesame*). *South* 50 (April 1984).

Dasenbrock, Reed Way. Review of *Close Sesame. World Literature Today* 59, 1 (1985), p. 147.

----------. "Creating a Past: Achebe, Naipaul, Soyinka, Farah." *Salmagundi* (Fall / Winter 1985-86), pp. 312-32.

Davidson, Basil. *Africa in Modern History*. Harmondsworth: Pelican, 1978.

De Lancey, Mark W., et al. *Somalia* («World Bibliographical Series» No. 92). Oxford: CLIO Press, 1988.

Durix, Jean-Pierre. "Through to Action" (review of *Close Sesame*). *The Times Literary Supplement* (16 December 1983), p. 1413.

----------. "Nuruddin Farah ou l'énigme de la liberté." *L'Afrique Litteraire et Artistique* 67 (1983), pp. 175-89.

----------. "Remapping the Motherland: *Maps*." *Third World Quarterly* 10, 4 (1988), pp. 1628-31.

Ekwe, Herbert. "A Weekend of African Literature." *Nigerian Guardian* (17 August 1986), p. 88.

Ewen, D. R. Review of *Sweet and Sour Milk. World Literature Written in English* 20, 2 (1981), pp. 221-24.

----------."Nuruddin Farah." In G. D. Killam (ed.), *The Writing of East and Central Africa*. London: Heinemann, 1984, pp. 192-210.

Fanon, Frantz. *Black Skin, White Masks*. Translated by Charles Lam Markmann. New York: Grove Press, 1961.

Finnegan, Ruth. *Oral Poetry*. Cambridge: Cambridge University Press, 1977.

Garscha, Karsten & Dieter Riemenschneider (eds.), *Afrikanischer Schriftsteller im Gespräch: Die Funktion Moderner Afrikanischer Literaturen*. Wuppertal: Hammer, 1983.

Gérard, Albert S. *African Language Literatures: An Introduction to the Literary History of Sub-Sahara Africa*. Washington, D.C.: Three Continents Press, 1981, pp. 155-60.

Glasse, Cyril. *The Concise Encyclopaedia of Islam*. London: Stacey International, 1989.

Gugler, Josef. "African Commentary on Dictators: Wole Soyinka's Plays and Nuruddin Farah's Novels." *Journal of Modern African Studies* 26, 1 (1988), pp. 171-77.

Herdeck, Donald E. "Nuruddin Farah." In his *African Authors: A Companion to Black African Writing Vol.1*. Washington, D.C.: Black Orpheus Press, 1973, p. 137.

Hinde, Thomas. "The Walls of Dawn" (review of *Sardines*). *Sunday Telegraph* (29 November 1981).

Holmes, E. S. "The Need for Preserving Somali Culture." *Ufahamu* 17, 2 (1989), pp. 6-9.

The Holy Qur'an: Text, Translation & Commentary, Vol.3. Translated by Abdullah Yusef Ali. Lahore: Sh. Muhammad Ashraf, 1980.

Hope, Christopher. "Boundaries of Desire: *Maps* by Nuruddin Farah." *New York Times Book Review* (15 November 1987), p. 40.

"Hufane," 'Umar Ma'allin. "The Voice of the Girls of the Horn of Africa." *Ufahamu* 17, 2 (1989), pp. 23-30.

Huggan, Graham. "Decolonizing the Map: Post-Colonialism, Post-Structuralism and the Cartographic Connection." *ARIEL* 20, 4 (1989), pp. 115-31.

Imfeld, Al & G. Meuer. "Nuruddin Farah: A Modern Nomad." *Afrika* 21, 9 (1980), pp. 23-25.

Kelly, Hilarie. "A Somali Tragedy of Political and Sexual Confusion: A Critical Analysis of Nuruddin Farah's *Maps*." *Ufahamu* 16, 2 (1988), pp. 21-37.

----------. "Commentary on Felix Mnthali 'Autocracy and the Limits of Identity.'" *Ufahamu* 17, 2 (1989), pp. 70-73.

Kidwai, S. Ahmed. "The Two Novels of Nuruddin Farah." In *Somalia and the World: Proceedings of International Symposium held in Mogadiscio, October 15-21, 1979*. Mogadiscio: State Press, 1980, pp. 191-201.

Kitchener, Julie. "Variations on a Theme" (review of *Close Sesame*). *New African* (December 1983), p. 52.

The Koran. Translated by N. J. Dawood, 1956; Fourth edition, Harmondsworth: Penguin, 1974.

Laitin, David D. & Said S.Samater. *Somalia: Nation in Search of a State*. Boulder: Westview Press, 1987.

Larson, Charles. "Third World Writing in English." *World Literature Today* 57, 1 (1983), pp. 58-59.

----------. "The Precarious State of the African Writer." *World Literature Today* 60, 3 (1986), pp. 409-13.

Laurence, Margaret. *A Tree for Poverty: Somali Poetry and Prose*. 1954. Dublin: Irish University Press, 1970.

Legum, Colin & Bill Lee. *Conflict in the Horn of Africa*. New York: Africana Publishing, 1977.

Lessing, Doris. "Oppressors" (review of *Close Sesame*). *New Society* (10 November 1983).

Lewis, I. M. *Peoples of the Horn of Africa*. London: International African Institute, 1965.

----------. *A Modern History of Somalia: A Nation and State in the Horn of Africa*. 1965. Revised & Expanded edition, Boulder & London: Westview Press, 1988.

----------. *Religion in Context: Cults and Charisma*. Cambridge: Cambridge University Press, 1986.

Lewis, Peter, "Closing the Cave" (review of *Close Sesame*). *London Magazine* 23, 11 (February 1984), pp. 101-05.

Lindfors, Bernth. "A Basic Anatomy of East African Literature." In David Dorsey, P. A. Egejunu & Stephen Arnold (eds.), *Design and Intent in African Literature*. Washington, D.C.: Three Continents, 1982, pp. 51-57.

----------. *Black African Literature in English 1982-1986*. London: Hans Zell, 1989.

Lowe, Colleen. "The Politician and the Writer Fuel Debate." *Kenya Times* (9 September 1983), p. 14.

Mbiti, John S. *African Religions and Philosophy*. London: Heinemann, 1969.

McCaughrean, Geraldine. *One Thousand and One Arabian Nights*. Oxford: Oxford University Press, 1982.

McEwan, Neil. *Africa and the Novel*. Atlantic Highlands: Humanities Press; London: Macmillan, 1983.

McHale, Brian. *Postmodern Fiction*. London & New York: Methuen, 1987.

Markakis, John. *National and Class Conflict in the Horn of Africa*. Cambridge: Cambridge University Press, 1987.

Mnthali, Felix. "Autocracy and the Limits of Identity: A Reading of the Novels of Nuruddin Farah." *Ufahamu* 17, 2 (1989), pp. 53-69.

----------. "A Reply." *Ufahamu* 17, 2 (1989), p. 74.

Moore, Gerald. "Personality and Heroism" (review of *Yussuf and His Brothers*). *West Africa* (16 August 1982), p. 2113.

----------. "Nomads and Feminists: The Novels of Nuruddin Farah." *International Fiction Review* 11, 1 (1984), pp. 3-12.

Morris, Patricia. "The Politics of Language." *African Concord* (14 August 1986), pp. 19-21.

Mumim, Sheikh Hassan. *Leopard Among the Women: Shabeelnaagood - A Somali Play*. Translated by B. W. Andrzejewski. London: Oxford University Press, 1974.

Nsar, Sayyed Hassein. *Ideals and Realities of Islam*. London: Allen & Unwin, 1985.

"Nuruddin Farah," in Daniel G. Marowski & Roger Matuz (eds.), *Contemporary Literary Criticism*. Detroit: Gale Research, 1989, pp. 131-41.

"Nuruddin Farah," in Hans Zell, Carol Bundy & Virginia Coulon (eds.), *A New Reader's Guide to African Literature*. London: Heinemann, 1983, pp. 386-88.

Okomilo, Ikhememho. "Power Game in Somalia" (review of *Sweet and Sour Milk*). *Africa* 101 (January 1980), pp. 72-73.

Okonkwo, Juliet I. "Nuruddin Farah and the Changing Roles of Women." *World Literature Today* 58, 2 (1984), pp. 215-21.

----------. "Nuruddin Farah and the Politics of Somalia." *Présence Africaine* 132 (1984), pp. 44-53.

----------. "Literature and Politics in Somalia: The Case of Nuruddin Farah." *Africa Today* 32, 3 (1985), pp. 57-65.

----------. "Farah and the Individual's Quest for Self-Fulfilment." *Okike* 26 (1986).

----------. "The Novelist as Artist: The Case of Nuruddin Farah." *Commonwealth Novel in English* 5, 1 (1992), pp. 46-58.

Ondaatje, Michael. *The English Patient*. 1992. London: Picador, 1993.

Oriere, Oje. "Politicians and Artists: Mouse Cat Relationship." *Sunday Standard* (Nairobi), (10 November 1985), p. 11.

Palmer, Eustace. "Two Views of Urban Life: Meja Mwangi, *Going Down River Road*; Nuruddin Farah, *A Naked Needle*." *African Literature Today* 9 (1978), pp. 104-08.

Petersen, Kirsten Holst. "The Personal and the Political: The Case of Nuruddin Farah." *ARIEL* 12, 3 (1981), pp. 93-101.

----------. "First Things Last: Problems of a Feminist Approach to African Literature." *Kunapipi* 6, 3 (1984), pp. 35-47.

Pilling, Jane. Review of *Sardines*. *Time Out* (4 December 1981).

Pullin, Faith. Review of *Sardines. British Book News* (Spring 1982), p. 320.

Rahman, Fazlur. *Islam and Modernity: Transformation of an Intellectual Tradition*. Chicago: University of Chicago Press, 1982.

Riesz, János. "Nuruddin Farah: Somalia's Literary Light." *World Press Review* (September 1981), p. 60.

----------. "Ein Kosmopolit aus Somalia: Das Werk des Schriftstellers Nuruddin Farah." *BAOBAB* 2 (1982), pp. 14-21.

----------. "Nachwort" in Nuruddin Farah, *Wie Eine Nackte Nadel* (*A Naked Needle*). Translated by Barbara Hillgen. Frankfurt: Lembeck, 1984, pp. 322-27.

Rirache, Mohamed Abdillahi. "Somali Poetry: The Case of the Miniature Genres." *Ufahamu* 17, 2 (1989), pp. 16-22.

Rushdie, Salman. *The Satanic Verses*. London: Viking, 1988.

----------. *Imaginary Homelands*. London: Granta, 1991.

Said, A. N. Review of *Sweet and Sour Milk. Horn of Africa* 4, 3 (1981), pp. 38-40.

Shrapnell, Norman. "In a Hell of a State" (review of *Sardines*). *The Guardian* (December 1981).

Samater, Said S. *Oral Poetry and Somali Nationalism: The Case of Sayyid Mohammad 'Abdille Hassan*. Cambridge: Cambridge University Press, 1982.

----------. "Oral Poetry and Political Dissent in Somali Society: The Hurgumo Series." *Ufahamu* 17, 2 (1989), pp. 31-52.

----------. "Nomad on the Nile." *Ufahamu* 17, 2 (1989), pp. 138-56.

Sander, Reinhard. Review of *A Naked Needle. World Literature Today* 53, 4 (1979).

Schraedeer, Peter. "The Novels of Nuruddin Farah: The Socio-Political Evolution of a Somali Writer." *Northeast African Studies* 10, 2-3 (1988), pp. 15-26.

Smith, Angela. "Nuruddin Farah." In D. L. Kirkpatrick & James Vinson (eds.), *Contemporary Novelists*. London & New York: St Martin's Press, 1986, pp. 278-79.

----------. *East African Writing in English*. London: Macmillan, 1989.

"Somalia." *Encyclopaedia of the Third World*, 2 Vols. New York: Facts on File, 1978, pp. 1301-1313.

"Somali Stories." Translated by B. W. Andrzejewski. In W. H. Whiteley (ed.), *A Selection of African Prose 1: Traditional Oral Texts*. Oxford: Clarendon, 1964, pp. 134-63.

Sontag, Susan. *Illness as Metaphor* and *Aids and Its Metaphors*. Harmondsworth: Penguin, 1991.

Sparrow, Fiona. "Telling the Story Yet Again: Oral Traditions in Nuruddin Farah's Fiction." *Journal of Commonwealth Literature* 24, 1 (1989), pp. 164-72.

Stewart, Desmond. *Early Islam*. The Hague: Time Life International, 1967.

Stratton, Florence. "The Novels of Nuruddin Farah." *World Literature Written in English* 25, 1 (1985), pp. 16-30.

Troughear, Tony. Review of *Sardines. Horn of Africa* 6, 1 (1983), pp. 50-52.

Turfan, Barbara. "Opposing Dictatorship: A Comment on Nuruddin Farah's *Variations on the Theme of an African Dictatorship*." *Journal of Commonwealth Literature* 24, 1 (1989), pp. 173-84.

Versi, Anver. "Farah's Mindscapes" (review of *Maps*). *New African* (May 1986), p. 65.

Vivan, Itala. "Chi e." *Nigrizia* (December 1984), p. 43.

Walmsley, Anne. "Nuruddin Farah and Somalia." *Index on Censorship* 10, 1-3 (1981), pp. 17-19.

Woolfson, Karen. "Writers in Conversation." *African Concord* (14 August 1986), pp. 18-19.

Wright, Derek. "Requiems for Revolutions: Race-Sex Archetypes in Two African Novels." *Modern Fiction Studies* 35, 1 (1989), pp. 55-68.

----------. "Parents and Power in Nuruddin Farah's *Dictatorship* trilogy." *Kunapipi* 11, 2 (1989), pp. 94-106.

----------. "Unwritable Realities: The Orality of Power in Nuruddin Farah's *Sweet and Sour Milk*." *Journal of Commonwealth Literature* 24, 1 (1989), pp. 185-92.

----------. "Somali Powerscapes: Mapping Farah's Fiction." *Research in African Literatures* 21, 2 (1990), pp. 21-34.

----------. "Zero Zones: Nuruddin Farah's Fiction." *ARIEL* 21, 2 (1990), pp. 21-42.

----------. "Oligarchy and Orature in the Novels of Nuruddin Farah." *Studies in Twentieth Century Literature* 15, 1 (1991), pp. 87-99.

----------. "Ethics and Ethnics in Nuruddin Farah's *Maps*." *New Researcher* 1 & 2 (1992), pp. 104-11.

----------. "Parenting the Nation: Some Observations on Nuruddin Farah's *Maps*." *College Literature* 19, 3 (1992) / 20, 1 (1993), pp. 76-84.

----------. "Fabling the Feminine in Nuruddin Farah's Novels." In Abdulrazak Gurnah (ed.), *Essays on African Writing: A Re-Evaluation*. Oxford: Heinemann, 1993, pp. 70-87.

----------. "Nuruddin Farah." In Eugene Benson & G. W. Connolly (eds.), *Routledge Encyclopaedia of Post-Colonial Literature*. London: Routledge, 1993.

----------. "Nations as Fictions: Postmodernism in the Novels of Nuruddin Farah." *Critique* 35, 2 (1994).

----------. Review of *Gifts. International Fiction Review* 22, 1 (1994).

----------. Review of *Gifts. World Literature Today* 68, 2 (1994).

Yeats, W. B. *Collected Poems*. London: Macmillan, 1967.

Theses and Dissertations

Ahmed, Ali Jimale. "Tradition, Anomaly and the Wave for the Future: Somali Oral Literature, Nuruddin Farah and Written Somali Prose Fiction." Ph.D., Queens College, City University of New York, 1990. *DAI* 50, 12 (1990), p. 3948A.

Mixon, Gloria. "The Social and Political Status of Women in thc Novels of Nuruddin Farah." M.A., University of Wisconsin, Madison, 1983.

Olagunji, John O. "The Role of Interior Monologue, Dialogue and Narrative in Selected Novels of Nuruddin Farah and Ayi Kwei Armah." M.A., University of Ibadan, Ibadan, Nigeria, 1985.

Oliver, Betty. "Patriarchy and Power: The Political Susceptibility of Islam in the Writing of Nuruddin Farah, with Particular Regard to the Position of Women." M.A., Northern Territory University, Darwin, Australia, 1992.

Bayreuth African Studies Series
Available Titles:

1 The Sudan: Ethnicity and National Cohesion
- Ethnicity, Regionalism and National Cohesion in the Sudan
- National Versus Regional: Methodological Problems in the Study of Nationalism and Nation Building in the Sudan
- The Dynamics of Ethnic Identification in Northern Dafur, Sudan

Price per title: DM 12,-

2 Towards African Authenticity
- The First African Novels in French: A Problem of Authenticity
- The Question of Ethnic Traditions Within a National Literature: The Example of Nigeria
- Early 20th Century Swahili Prose Narrative Structure and Some Aspects of Swahili Ethnicity
- The Development of Sierra Leone Krio

Price per title: DM 12,-

3 Littératures Africaines francophones
- Oralité, écriture et le problème de l'identité culturelle en Afrique
- Le concept de littérature nationale
- Au coeur de la littérature negro-africaine d'écriture française:

Price per title: DM 12,-

4 Approaches to African Identity
- Identity and the Political Economy of Islamic Conversion in Africa
- Difficultés de la notion d'universalité latérale
- Identity - Some Encouragements from a Psychological Perspective
- Identität in Gesetzgebung und Rechtsprechung in Afrika
- Identity and Socio-Economic Change in Nigeria - An Overview

Price per title: DM 12,- (out of print)

5 Language and Education in Africa
- Al-Hajj Sa'ad Umar Touré and Islamic Education Reform in Mali
- Conflicting Interests which Influence Hausa Women
- Sciences, techniques et cultures africaines
- English in Tanzanian Education
- Multilingualism and Language Policy in Sierra Leone

Price per title: DM 12,- (out of print)

6 Literature and African Identity
- Xenophobia and Class Consciousness in Recent Africa
- Literature and African Identity: The Example of Ayi Kwei Armah
- Is There a Nigerian Literature ?
- Le thème de l'identité culturelle dans le roman africain francophone

Price per title: DM 12,-

7 Drama and Theatre in Africa
- Offenheit und Beweglichkeit theatralischer Kommunikation in Afrika: Kulturelle Identitäten und internationale Aspekte
- Les origines d'un théâtre national africain: Le cas nigerian
- Radical Conservatism in Yoruba Popular Plays

Price per title: DM 12,-

8 Interviews avec des écrivains africains francophones

Interviews avec
- René Philombe
- Dono Ly Sangaré
- Amadou Koné
- Bernard Zadi Zaourou
- Jean Marie Adiaffi

Price per title: DM 12,-

9 Perspectives on African Music
- Afrikanische Musik, Ideologischer Kolonialismus und Identitätskrise der Zöglingsgeneration 1945-1970
- Musical Traditions, Islam and Cultural Identity in the Sudan
- Ebenezer Calender - An Appraisal
- Transcription and Translation of Calender's Repertoire List
- The Language and Content of Nigerian Popular Music
- Jambo Records and the Promotion of Popular Music in East Africa.

Price per title: DM 18,50

10 Douala 1893 - La Revolte des esclaves mercenaires

by **Adjai Paulin Oloukpona-Yinnon**

Price per title: DM 12,-

11 African and Western Legal Systems in Contact
- The Machinery of Justice in Nigeria
- The Impact of English Law Concepts on the Administration of Islamic Law in Nigeria
- The Changing Role of the Extended Family

Price per title: DM 12,-

12 Three Yoruba Artists
- Twins Seven-Seven
- Ademola Onibonokuta
- Muraina Oyelami

Price per title: DM 12,- (out of print)

13 Patterns of Language Knowledge and Language Use in Ngamiland in Botswana

by **Rainer Vossen**

Price per title: DM 12,-

14 KULANKULA - Interviews with Writers from Malawi and Lesotho
- Aubrey Kalitera
- Ken Lipenga
- Anthony Nazombe
- Njabulo S. Ndebele
- David Rubadiri

Price per title: DM 12,-

15 English in East and Central Africa I
- English in East Africa: Theoretical, methodological and practical issues
- Attitudes towards English among Kenyan students
- 'Non-Problematic Zambianisms' and their implications for the teaching of English in Zambia
- Second-language varieties across the Indian Ocean

Price per title: DM 12,-

16 Essays on Music in Africa 2
- Jùjú, Fúji and the Intercultural Aspects of Modern Yoruba Popular Music
- Concepts of Neo-African Music as Manifested in the Yoruba Folk Opera
- My Approach to Neo-African Music Theatre
- Intercultural Expressions in Neo-African Art Music

Price per title: DM 29,- (out of print)

17 New Religious Movements and Society in Nigeria
- The Quest for Identity in African New Religious Movements
- New Religious Movements and the Nigerian Social Order
- Spiritual Church Participation as a Survival Strategy
- Nationalistic Motifs in a Nigerian New Religious Movement

Price per title: DM 12,-

18 Linguistics in the Service of Africa

- Linguistics in the service of Africa: a retrospective view
- Researching into second language use and usage: with special reference to SeTswana in Ngamiland, Botswana
- Lexical problems of English in Africa
- Research into English and African languages in Nigeria
- A Corpus of East African English: prospects and problems
- English and African languages: excerpts from a discussion

Price per title: DM 12,-

19/20 Littérature et Politique en Afrique noire
by **Koffi Anyinefa**
Price per title: DM 39,-

21/22 Yoruba Drumming. The Dundun Tradition
by **Akin Euba**
Price per title: DM 59,-

23 Le Champs littéraire togolais
Edité par **János Riesz** et **Alain Ricard**

- Le champ littéraire togolais
- Génération Eyadema. Littérature populaire et littérature d'élite
- Firminger, Nachtigal, Zöller: trois témoins de la naissance du Togo (1884). A la recherche des premiers documents écrits de l'histoire togolais
- Sources allemandes sur l'histoire du Togo - 1884-1914
- Dietrich Westermann: pionnier de la recerche sur la culture ewe
- Entre littérature et propagande: les "Belles Lettres" coloniales allemandes sur le Togo
- Quand la littérature enjambe la frontière: "Amour de Féticheuse (au Dahomey et) au Togo" de Félix Couchoro
- Des écrivains et des langues: les Ewe qui écrivent
- La presse togolaise avant l'indépendance
- Le Togo diglossique? Proposition pour l'analyse d'une conscience linguistique au Sud du Togo
- Le palimpseste de l'écriture ouest-africaine francophone
- Agbebada meets Mister Tameklor. Un sujet, deux pièces de théâtre, trois générations: changement et continuité dans la société ewe
- La poésie togolaise en langue française. Réflexions sur l'"Anthologie de la poésie togolaise"

Price per title: DM 29,-

24 English in East and Central Africa 2
edited by **Josef Schmied**

- Deviation and language awareness in Kenyan popular literature
- Richer or rotten? A study of borrowing from English to Dholuo
- Establishing educational bilingual programmes in Tanzania: an alternative option
- Comprehension and sentence complexity in Tanzanian classrooms
- Assessing second language learner proficiency in Zambia
- Some grammatical sign-posts in Cameroon Standard English
- The role of English in education in Southern Africa

Price per title: DM 15,-

25 Akin Euba - An Introduction to the Life and Music of a Nigerian Composer
by **Joshua Uzoigwe**
Price per title: DM 19,80

26 Gros-Plan sur les femmes en Afrique / Afrikanische Frauen im Blick / Focus on Women in Africa
edited by **Gudrun Ludwar-Ene** and **Mechthild Reh**

- "Homme Nénuphar" - Discours amoureux et discours identitaire dans le poème "Latérite" de Véronique Tadjo
- *Kwantacce*, the 'Sleeping Pregnancy', a Hausa Concept
- The Social Relationships of Female and Male Migrants in Calabar, Nigeria: Rural Versus Urban Connections
- Industrieunternehmerinnen - Modell für einen Weg aus der ökonomischen Marginalisierung nigerianischer Frauen?
- Zur Problematik der Grundschulbildung für Mädchen in den ländlichen Regionen Nordkameruns
- Les activités des enfants dans les ménages abidjanais: A propos de la fonction socialisante du travail
- Macht und Religiöse Vielfalt im Norden Ugandas
- Protection of Widows and Administration of Customary Estates in Zambian Courts

Price per title: DM 29,-

27 Survey of Zimbabwean Writers. Educational and Literary Careers
by **Flora Veit-Wild**
Price per title: DM 29,-

28 Konflikte im kolonialen Alltag
by **Norbert Aas** and **Harald Sippel**
Price per title: DM 14,80

29 Intercultural Music I
edited by **Cynthia Tse Kimberlin** and **Akin Euba**
Price per title: about DM 39,-

30 Anglophone Cameroon Writing
edited by **Nalova Lyonga**, **Bole Butake** and **Eckhard Breitinger**
Price per title: DM 29,-

31 Theatre and Performance in Africa: Intercultural Perspectives
edited by **Eckhard Breitinger**
Price per title: DM 39,-

Prices do not include postage.

ALSO AVAILABLE:
Subsistence Cultivation, Market Production and Agricultural Development in Ruvuma Region, Southern Tanzania.
By **Doris Schmied**, (208 pp.) DM 29,-

The Sociolingiustic Impact of Kiswahili on Ethnic Community Languages in Tanzania: A Case Study of Ekinata
By **Rugatiri D.K. Mekacha**, (ca. 260 pp.) DM 29,-

Aspects of Interphonology: The Study of Kenyan Learners of Swahili
By **Paul Muthoka Musau**, (ca. 236 pp.) DM 29,-

FORTHCOMING:
Uganda. The Cultural Scenery
Edited by **Rose Mbowa & Eckhard Breitinger**, (ca. 230 pp.) DM 29,-

Orders for all titles to:
Eckhard Breitinger, University of Bayreuth, D-95440 Bayreuth, Germany
Tel. (0)921 - 55-3571; Fax: (0)921 - 55-3627; E-mail: Eckhard.Breitinger@btr0x1.hrz.uni-bayreuth.de